Write Your Family History Easy Steps to Organize, Save and Share

by

Stephen Szabados

Cover picture: My mom, sister and me circa 1953 (cousin's garden in Akron, Ohio)

Other Books by Author:

Finding Grandma's European Ancestors
Find Your Family History - Steps to get started
Polish Genealogy: Four steps to success
Basic Genealogy: Saving your family History
Memories of Dziadka
Polish Immigration to America: When, Where, Why and How
My Polish Grandmother
Hints for Translating Polish Genealogical Records
Deciphering the 1790-1840 U.S. Census Records: Two case studies

Copyright © 2014 Stephen M Szabados

Kindle Direct Publishing Platform

All rights reserved.

11/05/2018

ISBN: 1495442691
ISBN-13: 978-1495442698

DEDICATION

For my children and grandchildren and their reading enjoyment

CONTENTS

CHAPTER ONE - WHY WRITE YOUR FAMILY HISTORY 1

CHAPTER TWO – START YOUR RESEARCH 7

CHAPTER THREE – SOURCES OF INFORMATION 13

CHAPTER FOUR – EVALUATING 45

CHAPTER FIVE – MORE ABOUT WRITING 53

CHAPTER SIX – BEYOND THE BASICS: 67

CHAPTER SEVEN – PUBLISHING YOUR FAMILY HISTORY 87

CHAPTER EIGHT – MY FINAL THOUGHTS ON 93

APPENDIX A – MY FAMILY HISTORY PAGES 95

APPENDIX B – LULU.COM EXAMPLE 111

APPENDIX C – USEFUL BOOKS AND WEBSITES 133

INDEX 137

ACKNOWLEDGMENTS

There are a few people that I need to recognize for their help with this book.

Jennifer Holik was a huge help with the early and final draft of this book. Her comments helped organize my material into a format that was more readable and make it a useful tool.

I also need to express my appreciation to Teresa McMillin for her advice and comments for the chapter on Genealogical Proof and Citing Sources. Her expertise was a tremendous help in clarifying a difficult topic.

Joan Huff and her years of experience in genealogy were a tremendous help in the final editing. I rely on her years of experience to keep me on the right track.

I cannot forget my loving wife Susan who deserves my love for her patience and her efforts with the editing of this book.

INTRODUCTION

Genealogy research should go beyond finding documents and filling in charts. This book outlines a simple process that will aid your research and create pages of information that can be read and understood by all family members. Your research will become faster and more accurate and your family can enjoy the family history.

We all have family stories that give insights into the lives of our ancestors. Some are entertaining, others are celebrations of our cultural heritage and others are more historical in nature. They all should be saved so they can accurately pass down to future generations.

You may find it hard to believe that your family history is important to save. You should consider that all of our immigrant ancestors contributed to America's history and their stories should be saved for our grandchildren. The farmers and the factory workers contributed their efforts to the growth of America alongside all of the names listed in the history books. Our family histories should give clues of their roles and this will help us understand our roots.

Your collection of family oral histories, photos and documents are incomplete unless someone writes an explanation of how they are related. This creates your unique family history and is the core of why someone needs to write them down for the enjoyment of your children and grandchildren. You may be reluctant to capture these stories because you do not consider yourself a writer. This can seem to be a very challenging project for many people. If you feel you do not have the skills to do this, who in your family can? If you like to do the research, is there someone that can work with you to write it? It is important to understand that someone in your family should capture and save the oral histories now before the stories are further diluted or lost completely.

I also find it difficult to write. However, I began creating summaries for the individuals that I was researching and I used these as quick reference pages. When I discovered that these short summaries could easily be read by other family members, the summaries were slowly expanded to create my family history.

If you are interested in telling your family stories, I hope that the materials in this book will help you overcome your fears of writing and you will commit your family story to the written word. I show how getting started with brief biographical summaries can make writing easier and overcome your fears of writing, I cover simple methods for organizing your summaries that can stand alone and then later be combined into a larger document that becomes your family history.

The book reviews a simple process that compiles oral history, family pictures and genealogical documents and puts it together into a readable and interesting document that suddenly becomes your family history.

Writing Your Family History

Don't be afraid to begin. Concentrate on finding one story and then another by doing the research. Finding the small pieces will make the task easier and will be fun. Eventually the small pieces will begin to fit together and the overall story that is your family history will appear.

My focus in the early stages in writing my family history was the research and identifying the stories that my relatives, documents and pictures told. My focus was not writing the history. The summaries that were the basis for the history were written to help with my research and to help share the information with my family. As I connected with family members, groups of summaries were merged together to share information about their ancestors. Over time the merged groups of summaries were combined and organized in one large document that became the family history that was published and distributed to the family members. As you can see, the family history came together almost by accident. This method put very little pressure on me to produce such an important document. There was a lot of work to do the research and keep the summaries updated but the final document seemed to emerge and cry out to be published. Also note that the summaries and documents could also stay in the ring binders and not be published. The ring binder will still be organized enough for someone in the future to pickup and continue your work. However, publishing your work gives the family more copies of your work and more chances that your work will survive and be available for someone to continue your work.

A family history should be based on thorough and sound research; identify what is included that is fact and what are conclusions; tell stories of our ancestors; be well organized in content and presentation; document all facts that are included (cite your sources); includes family documents and pictures

A family history can be a great treasure to you, your family and future generations. It can help us understand our heritage both here in the U.S. and where our ancestors came from. It lets us gain knowledge and appreciation for our ancestors and their lives.

Whichever path you choose, do the work so it can be organized and saved to be used by future generations. Get the details and do the work so that it's worth saving.

Do it now!

CHAPTER ONE - WHY WRITE YOUR FAMILY HISTORY

Why write your family history?

I have always wanted to know more about my family's history. However, I began my genealogical research after my parents and grandparents had died. This was a handicap but this was soon forgotten after I found my first documents. I quickly became addicted to genealogy research.

Once I began compiling the information from oral history and documents, I realized that family histories are more than piles of documents that list parents, grandparents and their ancestors. Our family histories are made up of the stories that can be found in the oral histories, the pictures and the documents. I found that I became more excited about my history as the stories developed on how these pieces of information were related. I also discovered that my initial view of my family changed quickly as the information and stories flowed from the documents. As more information was found, my family history gave me a greater closeness to my ancestors and their lives. Identifying who, what and where that were represented in family photo albums will pass along the memories that my ancestors tried to capture in these photos. Interpreting the facts shown on the various documents and explaining their relationship in the lives of my ancestors brought my pages to life. This was important because only a few people enjoy doing the research and then interpreting the documents. However, most family members enjoy reading the stories. Our task is to find a way to save our family history in a format that can be enjoyed by most family members.

Uncovering our history should remind us of our roots. Writing about the major events in the lives of our ancestors helps us and our descendants understand how our ancestors affected our lives. All of our immigrant ancestors made significant contributions to America's history. They may not be mentioned in history books but their efforts were needed for the growth of America. Think about the work that was needed by the early settlers to clear the land and establish their first homes. Think about the many immigrants that were needed to fuel the industrial growth in America.

Compiling documents and pictures in a ring binder is a standard method of organizing genealogy research. However, I realized that I wanted to save my research in a better format that could be read and understood easily. The pages that I left behind had to contain the stories in my family history. A pile of pictures and an album of pictures could depict many aspects of family history but they must be interpreted and their relationships should be written down.

Writing down the stories and the relationships helps us understand our heritage and the lives our ancestors. After sharing my results with other family members, I get a sense that our family has become more connected. This will also preserve the memories of our ancestors for our future generations. Creating a written family history should also help future generations feel more connected to our ancestors. Writing a family history should also preserve what our efforts uncovered. My goal is to leave my research in a format that future researchers can fully understand what I found and use it as a starting point to further expand it.

Start now to write a family history. This will help preserve the accuracy of your stories as they are now. The next chapter of this book will cover a method that starts with small steps that will slowly develop into a wonderful history that can be treasured by many future generations. Do not procrastinate. The longer you wait, the more likely you will lose older family members who die or suffer memory loss before they can pass along their valuable family memories. Also remember that once you start you will never finish gathering family information. Share your work periodically with your family and join with them when their enjoyment is revealed.

Find the time to get started. Even a few minutes daily or weekly can make a difference.

Need to preserve Oral History

Family histories usually include many oral histories. They are an important method of how family histories are passed down to each generation. However, I realized that oral history is not the best method to accurately preserve our history. I saw the following potential problems:

- Some facts may be missed in the oral history when told by different people.
- Some facts may be added or embellished by various story tellers.
- Some facts are lost as memories fade.
- Some oral history is lost as we lose our older relatives before their stories can be recorded.

One example is the story of my father's military service:

On July 11, 1942, my father enlisted in the Army Air Corps. However his folder at the St Louis records facility for military records was destroyed in a fire in July of 1973 so many details of his service have been lost.
- *His brother told me that my father was a bombardier/nose gunner.*
- *He was discharged from the military on September 10, 1943 after only 14 months of service. When I asked about his early discharge, he indicated that my father injured his back during a crash landing after a bombing mission.*
- *My father did tell me that his back pain was due to an injury that was caused during a plane crash while he was in the Army Air Corps.*

Some of this story is true and some facts are contradicted by his discharge papers.
- Fact - He was discharged while training at an airfield in Utah
- Confirmation - His discharged papers listed the reason for his discharge was due to not being able to physically perform his duties (this probably was due to his back injury)
- Contradiction - He did not see any combat
- Contradiction - His rating at the time of his discharge was as a mechanic
- Confirmation – Photos indicated that he was stationed at an airfield near the desert which may have been Las Vegas. This was the first facility that was setup for gunnery training
- Confirmation - Photos did show that he had earned his wings which meant that he was a member of the flight crew (he probably was the substitute gunner for a flight crew with mechanic being his main task)

My conclusions from interpreting all of the sources are:
I believe my father was a member of a flight crew as a substitute gunner on a B-25 bomber but his primary job was as a mechanic. He was in the final stages of his training when he was injured in a crash landing in Utah. His back injury from this crash disqualified him from further service and he was honorably discharged from the Army Air Corps after fourteen months of service.

Why Write Your Family History

As you can see it would be easy for my memories of my conversations with my father and uncle to be lost if I did not write them down. Also I feel that my knowledge of the oral history and access to the photo albums gives me better insight and ability to interpret what I found. Future generations would have access to the same documents and pictures but would not have the same insight.

Below are a portion of the pictures from my mother's photo album that I used to come to my conclusions of my father's service. The document shown in the lower right corner is a copy of a portion of my father's discharge papers that indicated his rank and classification at discharge and that he had not seen combat.

Historical pictures and an Air Force friend identifies the building as a barracks at Sheppard Field, Wichita Falls, Texas

The street sign helped identify the location. Also note that he is wearing airman wings

The cactus may indicate that this was taken near Las Vegas. Also note that he is wearing airman wings

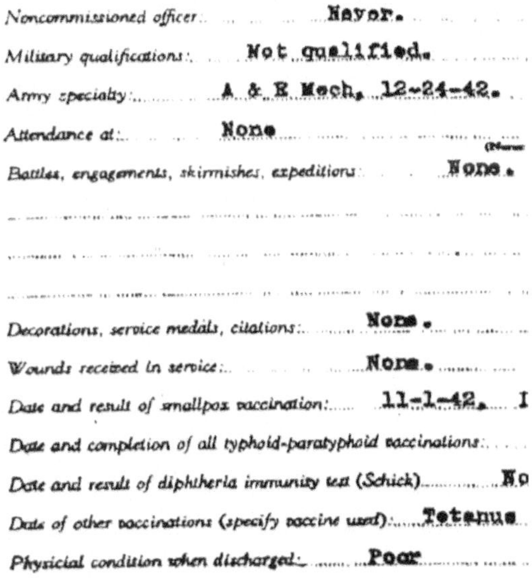

Portion of his discharge papers that indicate that he was discharged in poor health as a mechanic and had seen no combat,

Early Problems

My initial attempts to share my research at family gatherings were disappointing. These early efforts were using a ring binder with tabs for each ancestor and copies of the documents that I had found. I had not begun using summaries. Most relatives were not interested in reviewing documents and charts. They found the documents hard to read and the charts difficult to understand.

To improve the experience at future family gatherings, I tried to find a better format to present the material. I reviewed various lineage software reports but I could not find any that suited my requirements. The only software report that I found somewhat acceptable to my methods was the "Smart Stories" available with the Family Tree Maker software. This feature created a word document from the genealogical facts and notes that had been entered for a person. The Smart Story could be edited as a word document and had the ability to insert pictures and documents. However, if future research changed the basic genealogical data a new smart story had to be created which included the need to reinsert all pictures and documents. This new "Smart Story" did not carry over the documents and pictures that were added to the previous smart story. This problem limits my usage of the Smart Story option. I do use this feature to create my initial summary for a person. However, after I have edited and inserted documents and pictures, I begin using this work as my summary. If I revise genealogical data in Family Tree Maker, I use this as a filing cabinet but do not create any new Smart Stories for that individual. My summary is revised manually with any new information.

I settled on using word documents as the main organizing tool for my genealogy research because this allowed me flexibility in how the information was presented and I could add pictures and documents to explain what was written. I create summaries for each individual to be included in the family history. This generally means direct ancestors. Siblings of a direct ancestor are also included but they are listed as a group after their father. This group listing also includes a short summary for each sibling that includes a list of their children but does not extend to their grandchildren. I research siblings of my direct ancestor because many events in their lives may mirror the life of my ancestor. Documents for the sibling may list facts about the family that may not be found on documents for my direct ancestor.

Initially these summaries are edited and saved as separate documents for each ancestor. I have shared these summaries with relatives and sent them copies of my pages. If the shared information is for a number of ancestors, I merge the individual summaries and then save and send this a one combined document. At this point, I begin using the larger combined document as my primary summary. Eventually all of the individual summaries have been merged into one large document. Step by small step I am creating my family history book.

What is holding you back?

Writing your family history should be a by-product of genealogical research but I have found four reasons that genealogy researchers give to explain why they have not started their family histories.

1. **The first reason is "I have no idea on where to start."**
   This is probably the easiest myth to answer. My answer is "It does not matter where you start." I recommend starting with a person such as a parent or grandparent where many facts are already known. I believe the best place to start would be with the person you feel the most comfort talking about. Once you get started researching the first person, researching for the other people in your family tree will become easier.

   Remember that your family history is compiled by researching individuals. The stories of each individual are related to other members of the family. One person's story will help you find facts for other members of the family. These may be siblings, parents or children. As the story for each individual unfolds, you will start to see a bigger picture and this will develop into your family history.

2. **Another reason used to delay writing family histories is "I am too busy or I am having difficulty finding the time to just do my research."**
Most people feel that they are busy and they cannot add new activities. Finding copies of documents for the ancestors takes up all of the time that they have for genealogy and they do not have the time to write down the information found in the documents.

My instincts told me that I had to be organized to wade through the mountain of documents that I was finding. This led to a method that made more research more efficient. I tried to get my research organized into folders in my filing cabinet but the real key to better research for me was when I began compiling the facts that I found into summaries. This gave me a quick reference when I needed certain facts to do more research for an ancestor. Once I started doing my summaries, I began finding more information faster. I used the same amount of time as I had before but my research gave me more results. Another benefit was that my information was more readable to the non-genealogist in the family. When I shared my research with family members in this new readable format, I began receiving more information and documents from my family. When I step back and look at what I have done, I realize that writing the summaries not only helped me do a better job researching the facts but that the summaries were the initial phase of my written family history.

3. **The next reason I hear is "I am waiting to finish my research before I start writing because I want to make sure I have the complete story."**
Why wait? We will never be finished writing our family history because new information is being found and made available every day. New databases are found and you meet more relatives. You will never finish gathering family information or researching your ancestors, so don't put off writing.

Do not procrastinate getting started. The longer you wait, the more likely it will be that older family members may die or lose their memory before passing along the memories that could be so valuable for you.

Sharing a readable document with family members will also get you more stories, pictures and documents to add to the history.

Start recording your history now. Do it when the information is fresh in your mind. It will make you more efficient, you will find more information and by sharing it you will be able to enjoy it more with your family.

4. **The last reason is "I am not a writer."**
Most people find writing intimating and I am not an exception. Writing assignments in high school and college were challenging for me but I think I have found a trick. It has made it easier for me to start my writing.

My trick is that I use bullet points when I start recording facts for an ancestor. This helps me quickly record the facts that I find and I do not have to worry about the rules of grammar. I do try to minimize spelling mistakes but I am careful to enter names as found on the documents even if the name seems to be incorrect.

Here is an example of simple bullet point entries:
- *John Read was born in 1604 in Canterbury, Kent, England.*
- *He married Sarah Lessie.*
- *Sarah Lessie was born in 1614 in Blyborough, Lincolnshire, England.*
- *She died on April 23, 1702 in Rehoboth, Bristol, Massachusetts.*
- *John died on September 7, 1685 in Rehoboth, Bristol, Massachusetts.*

Note that using bullet points are a great help to me when I start compiling information. It helps to get the words flowing and not worry about the quality of the writing. Experienced writers do numerous rewrites and I also use this method. As I enter new information, I review what I have previously written and keep revising my work. I also add my source information and make the overall information more readable for other people. This last step is much easier to the non-writer after you begin to get into the flow of writing. Taking small steps helps me construct the pieces that will eventually be the family history. My focus is not the larger history but the research and the updating of the individual summaries.

Summary:

My initial genealogical research was to satisfy my desires to know more about my family. Once I started finding documents and piecing the stories together, I added the desire to save my family history for my children and grandchildren.

I found that my research became faster and more efficient when I started to compile the information into individual summaries for each ancestor. The summaries made it faster to look up information needed to do additional research and they make sharing your research easier.

CHAPTER TWO – START YOUR RESEARCH AND GET ORGANIZED

The initial part of writing a family history is the search for oral histories, pictures and documents that will tell you the stories that will become your family history. To increase the chances to be successful in your research, you will need to be organized and organizing your genealogy research should go beyond developing storage and filing systems for your notes, pictures and documents.

The main aspect of getting organized should be saving the information that you find in your research. The information related to your family history should to be compiled from the oral history, pictures and documents that you find. Documents and pictures should be organized and safely stored away but the information found in the documents is the more important aspect of your research. Any information that are found should be analyzed for accuracy and all the information correlated into the story that will be your family history. Also note that organizing your information will help you find more information and your summaries will show what information is missing.

I begin organizing my research by using standard genealogy charts to capture the relationships and the names of family members. I also start writing a summary for each direct ancestor. In the summaries I include all the information that I find in the documents. Each document is a snap shot of the life of an ancestor and I try to capture each detail indicated in the document. This method helps me gather, correlate, and analyze my information. I also make sure that each entry identifies where I found each fact. Including the source helps me draw better conclusions about the accuracy of my information and also helps me find clues that point to more sources.

When I begin researching a family, I usually start with a parent or a grandparent because they normally are the people we know the most about My first source of information is the oral histories from family members. The names of ancestors and their children are recorded on ancestry and family group charts. I use lineage software to help keep track the relationships. Next, I review documents, letters and photos that I find in the shoe boxes and desk drawers. At this stage, I summarize the information and then start searching online databases.

One important benefit that I enjoy from my summaries is that they make my research efforts more efficient. Information that I needed to continue my research was more readily available and using summaries have allowed me to find information faster.

Using a ring binder with tabs is one method that I have used to store my summaries, photos and documents. The ring binder is an efficient format to have the information available when doing more research and it is also an excellent way to share my research at family gatherings.

I do not include the originals of documents and photos in the ring binder. Original documents may be old and fragile. They should be stored in a safe location using archival materials and handled infrequently.

The picture shows a relative enjoying the summaries at a family gathering

Genealogy Charts

Here is an example of my family tree using Family Tree Maker software. Note that the view shows both the pedigree chart (top) and the Family Group (bottom). I use this as a quick reference to refresh my memory about relationships

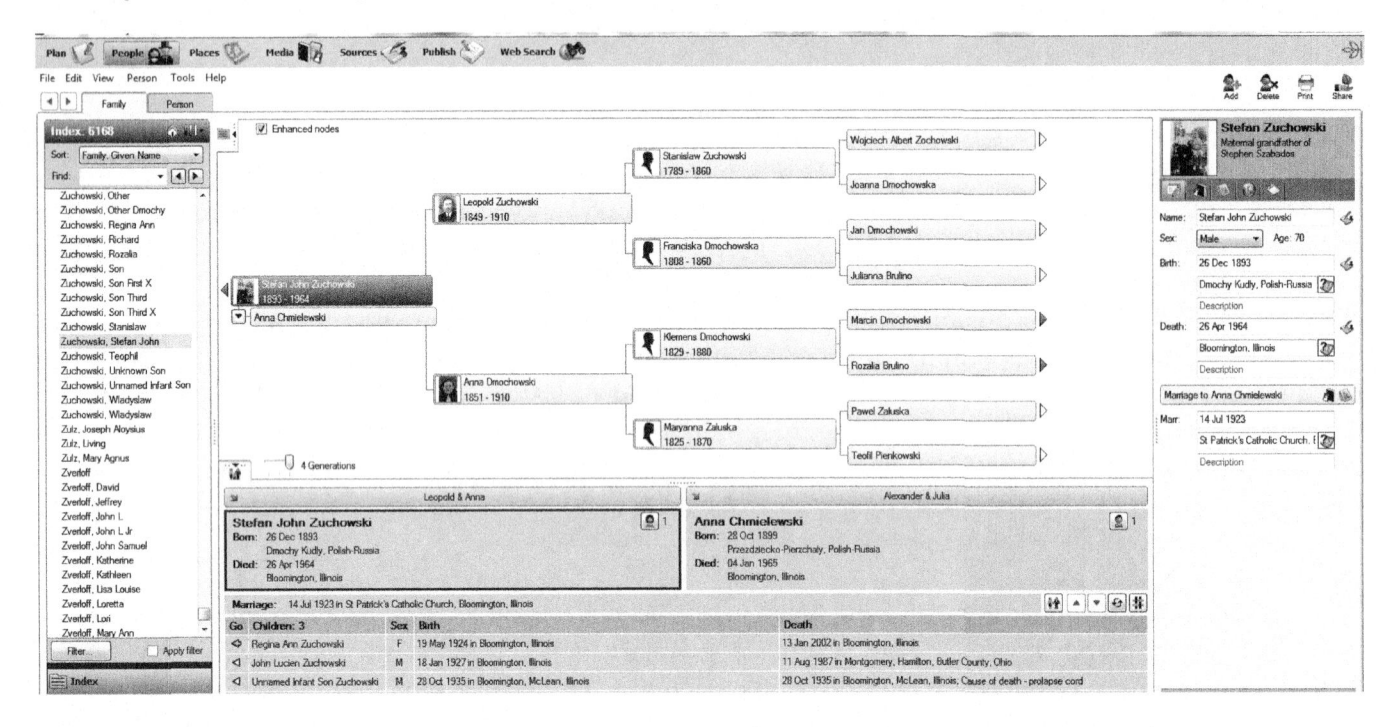

Research Log

Another helpful tool when doing genealogy research is a research log. The log should include notes about when I did specific searches and what I found or did not find and what source I used. Research logs are important because they help me avoid duplicate searches.

Sample format for Research Log

Research Log

Ancestor:

Date	Place of Research	Purpose	Source	Results

Format of my Summary

Below is the template that I use for my summaries of individual ancestors. Note that this list is in chronological order and contains items such as immigration information that may not apply to all people. This list is given as a suggestion for you to use. Items can be added and deleted as you feel they are needed.

- Birth information - Date, birthplace and names of parents
- Marriage – Date, place and name of spouse and children
- Immigration - Departure and arrival dates, name of ship, what ports did they depart and arrive, name of person they left and their destination – who and where
- Addresses of all residences plus when they lived there (use census records, city directories and addresses found on documents such as children's birth certificates
- What was their occupation and where did they work
- Education – Names of schools, their highest grade completed, their activities and honors
- Hobbies
- Names of friends
- Achievements
- Death - When and where
- Where they are buried
- Pictures of ancestors, family, residences, churches, schools, place of work, gravesite
- Documents

Below is an example of a few items from my grandfather's summary. Note that each bullet point lists the information that I found in a specific document. Another important hint is that I included the name of the document and where I found it. (I underlined the source to illustrate this point for you but I do not underline the source in my histories.) The next step in my process is to include the copy of the document after the summary. In this case, I have included a copy of Steve's baptismal certificate. The label for the document will list where the copy came from. After Steve's baptismal record, I show you a copy of his father's birth record from the church register. I show this document because the record is in Polish and I try to include a translation to English for documents in a foreign language.

Her is a portion of Summary for Steve Zuchowski:
- His baptismal certificate listed that he was born in Dmochy Kudly, Russia on December 26, 1893 to Leopold Zuchowski and Anny Dmochowska.
- Steve's passenger manifest listed that at age 19; he boarded the steamship SS Rhein in Bremen and departed for America on October 3, 1912. (Note that the Ancestry.com index for the manifest has Steve listed as Jan Lackowski). His occupation on the passenger manifest was listed as farmer. The SS Rhein arrived in Philadelphia on October 16, 1912. The passenger manifest listed his final destination as his brother Boleslaw Zuchowski at 1217 W Monroe St in Bloomington, Illinois.

A larger example of one my family histories can be seen in Appendix A.

Saving the Documents

Below is a copy of my great-grandfather's birth record from Poland. Note that I listed that it can be found on film number 939453 from the Family History Center catalog. Also note that the record is in Polish and I included an English translation for my family members as they read my family history.

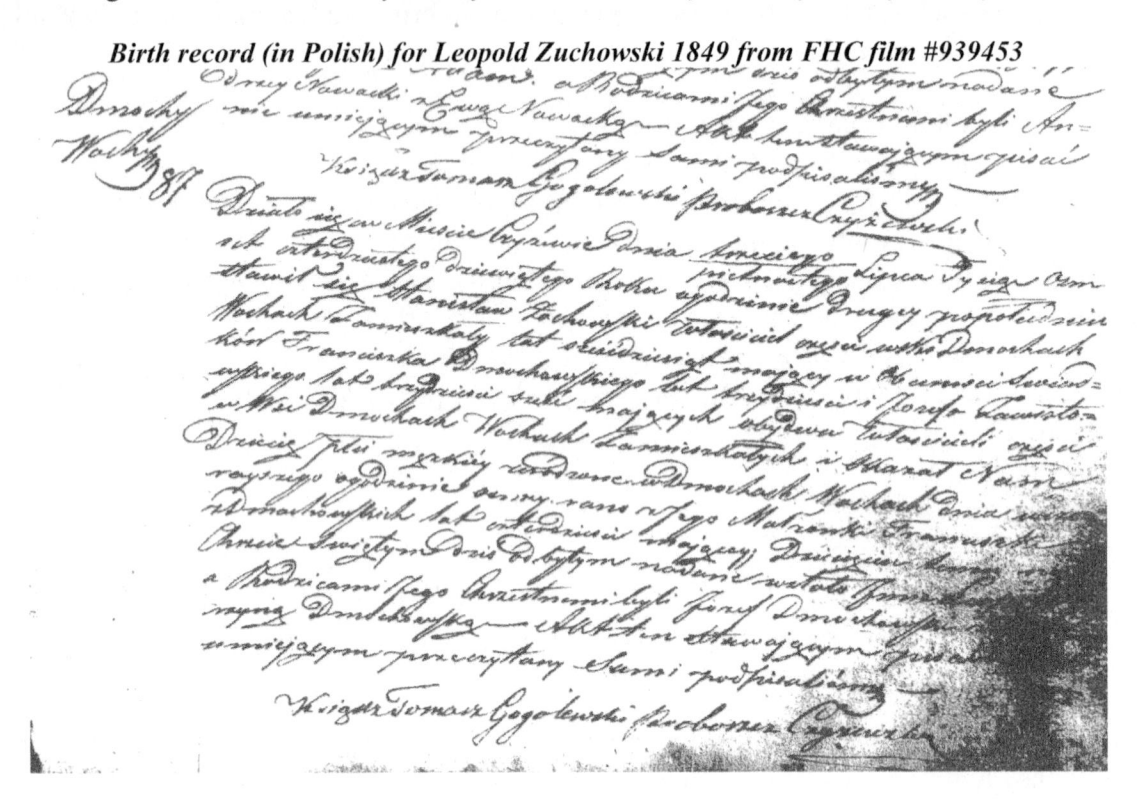

Birth record (in Polish) for Leopold Zuchowski 1849 from FHC film #939453

Translation of Leopold's baptismal record:
It took place in the town of Czyzew on the third day of July and was baptized on the fifteenth in 1849 at two o'clock in the morning. Stanislaw Zochowski presented himself land owner in village of Dmochy Wochy of Lomza district at sixty years of age in the presence of witnesses Franciszka Dmochowska age 30 and Josefa Zawistowska age 36 both living in the village of Dmochy Wochy. He show us the child of male sex born in Dmochy Wochy on this day at the eighth hour of the morning from his wife Franciszka Dmochowska forty years of age and that he wished to give the child the name of Leopold with godparents Jozef Dmochowski and …… rzyna (probably Kataryna) Dmochowska. This document was read to all present and signed by Reverend Tomasz Godlewski Pastor of Czyzew

My summaries help me organize information and then see what information is missing. The format of my summaries makes the exchange of information with others easier. I try to show my work to as many relatives as possible. My ring binders include pictures, oral histories and documents that I share with everyone. Reading the summaries and seeing the pictures, stories and documents help open up the memories of everyone. Besides making it easier for relatives to remember family stories, the ring binders show everyone how serious my research is and makes it comfortable for them to exchange copies of documents and pictures.

The more people that see your work, the more additional stories, documents and pictures you will dig out of the closets of your relatives. This is one of the benefits of writing your family history as you do your research rather than wait.

Start Your Research and Get Started

Below is an email that I received from a relative who shared many documents, pictures and additional information with me for the family history. The files attached to the email were the first installment of information that he shared. Some of the documents that he shared were carried by the grandparents when they immigrated. These documents helped lead the way to their Bohemian village and they helped find the Bohemian records that describe the family before they emigrated. (note that I substituted XXXX for some of the names for privacy reasons)

From: XXXX12@comcast.net
To: "Szabados, Steve" <s-szabados@sbcglobal.net>

9 Files View Slideshow Download All img389.jpg (421KB); img390.jpg (343KB); img391.jpg (572KB); img392.jpg (1786KB); img393.jpg (1796KB); img394.jpg (481KB); img395.jpg (830KB); img396.jpg (1426KB); img397.jpg (1295KB)

Steve, this is great you put a lot of work into this. Here's some stuff from XXXXXX. My mom and dad's wedding was May 5, 1945. The one picture you have next to Aunt XXXX and Uncle XXX in Mexico is Uncle XXX and Aunt XXXX. The picture you have with my dad and Uncle XXXX as kids is my dad and his best friend XXXXX. The picture you have in front of the candy store that says its XXX to the far right is not XXX I don't know who it is. My mom's maiden name is XXXXX. The pictures of the brothers and sisters when they were kids are great I've never seen them before. I never knew much about Uncle XXXX maybe that's why there is still a cigar making machine in the basement. I know him and Uncle XXX worked for the railroad. Uncle XXXXX worked in the tower on 29th and Kedzie right around the corner from where they lived and Uncle XXXXXX was in a shack along the railroad tracks on 31st street next to the Cook County jail they were switchmen. I'll probably find more stuff.

Sample of one of the documents received in the above email This is a copy of the birth record for the immigrant that they obtained when they left

Summary on organizing and starting your research

Begin documenting your research by recording information found in documents into summaries for each ancestor. Include labeled pictures with your documents and try to identify who are in the pictures and when was the picture taken. Keep a research log for each ancestor. Record, correlate, and analyze information in your summaries to help identify sources. Cite the source of your information If you use a computer to write your history, remember to back up your work often. After all your hard work and effort, it would be very frustrating to lose the information because of a computer failure.

CHAPTER THREE – SOURCES OF INFORMATION

Stories at family gatherings were probably your first source of family history information. After your grandparents or parents died, you gained access to shoe boxes of documents and pictures in closets and desk drawers full of documents. These initial pieces of information will set the foundation for your genealogy records and today there are many more sources that you can use to research and to expand your family history.

After I have review all the shoe box documents and I have interviewed all of the living relatives, I begin searching for more records on the internet, libraries and historical archives. However, before you start searching for more records; please remember that some of the information that you have and will find may be confusing, misleading and wrong. To overcome these confusing records, you have to remember you need to always analyze your information and interpret what you find. Does the information make sense and is there corroborating information in other documents. Evaluating data as you find the documents will help keep you on the right track of finding your ancestors. If you use erroneous data you will waste time researching people that are not in your family.

Another facet to remember is that some information that you find may be embarrassing but you cannot change it. You have to accept what you find and include it in your family history. Then continue your search one generation at a time.

Now let's cover some of the non-family sources and types of records. In the following pages I will cover the various documents that I have found useful in expanding family histories. I will try to list the information each document may include. Please remember that formats of these documents will change over the years and vary by location. Some formats may contain the data that I list but other formats may include less or some even list more details. Having flexibility to deal with these variations is part of the challenge of genealogical research.

Census Records

After oral history and personal documents, the next source that I use to find family history is census records. These records are a snapshot of your family at the time the census was taken and contain a wealth of information that can be used in your family histories.

The U.S. Federal Census was mandated in 1787 by the U.S. Constitution to count the U.S population to determine representation in the U.S. House of Representatives. The U.S. Constitution required that the census should be done in 1790 and every ten years thereafter. You may also find that state census records can be used the same as the federal records although they may show less information.

For the genealogist, census records are more than a list of individuals. Generally I recommend that you start with the 1940 federal census or the latest census before your ancestor's death and work backward in time. After I have identified the parents and siblings, I record all other personal information that I can find on these records. The 1850 through 1940 federal census records list a great deal of personal information about your family. They are a picture of your family and can be a treasure trove of information. The format for each year changed but the various census records listed information on place of residence, names of the people in the household with their ages and gender, what year was the couple married, where were they born, where were their parents born, when did they immigrate, were they naturalized, could they read or write and their occupation. Also noting what was the date the census information was recorded is important when accounting for births, marriage and deaths of people missing on the record but who you thought should have been listed.

The format of the census records for 1790 through 1840 required listing only basic information that was needed to give the Federal government an accurate head count and these were used primarily to establish the boundaries for the congressional districts. These early census records included the names of only the head of the household, state, county, and town, counts of the household by age ranges and gender, and the number of slaves by gender. Between 1800 and 1840, officials slowly added demographic information such as the ability to read and write and the types of industry where they worked.

States and territories also conducted censuses. Some were merely head counts but some had very useful genealogical information that could be very important for your family history. A state census usually was not taken in the same year as the federal census records and therefore may show different facts. Find as many census records as possible and get as many snapshots of your family as possible.

Below is an example of how I use census information. The portion of one of my summaries that is shown uses the addresses found on documents to find or take photos of the homes which I feel gives more insight to the neighborhood where they lived and brings more life to family histories

Portion of summary for Andrzy Dombrowski:
- The 1900 Federal census listed that Andrzy, Julia and children lived in Chicago at 661 Holt (now 1402) and Andrzy was working as a tanner.
- In the 1907 Chicago City Directory, Andrew is living at 379 W Armitage (now 2130) and working as a tanner.
- For the 1910 and 1920 census listed the family at 2130 Armitage plus the 1920 census lists that daughter Mary is living in the upper unit of the two flat at 2130 W Armitage with her husband Frank Rybka and their daughter Virginia.
- From 1900 to 1920, Andrzy worked as a tanner at a nearby leather factory. Andrzy retired in 1920.

661 Holt now 1402 Greenview | 2130 Armitage (2008 photo with front modernized)

More Information

City & Farm Directories

City directories and farm directories can be found for some areas. They are listings of residents, streets, businesses, organizations or institutions, giving their location and usually occupation. Sometimes their employer is listed. They predate telephone directories and they have been in use for centuries. They generally only list those persons who are employed in the house but also may list spouses in parenthesis. Although directories do not list the wealth of data that census records have, directories are still a small snapshot of your family.

Sample showing a page from the 1891 Bloomington Illinois City Directory

People's Bank, Bloomington. Capital $100,000. Surplus $80,000. Directors, P. Whitmer, L. Ferre, H. Capen, G. F. Dick, A. E. Stevenson, H. M. Senseney, J. Keenan.

CITY DIRECTORY. 417

Scanlan John, condr C & A, res 914 W Locust.
Scanlan Lizzie C, res 1316 N Ewing.
Scanlan Mary E Miss, bkkpr M Livingston, res 1316 N Ewing.
Scanlan Patrick, lab C & A roundhouse, res 1316 N Ewing.
Scanlan Simon, res 1316 N Ewing.
Scanlan Wm T, porter F Oberkoetter & Co, res 706 E Washington.
Schaefer Louis, painter, res 514 S Lee.
Schaefer John, paperhanger, res 514 S Lee.
Schaeffer Bernhardt, shoemkr, 605 N Lumber, res same.
Schaeffer Carl L (Niergarth & Schaeffer), res 609 N Main

JOHNSON The Grocer AND Commission Merchant

The best and largest variety at lowest prices. Will not be undersold by any house in city or county for same class of goods.

125, 127, 129 E Beaufort St.

NORMAL, ILL.

W-B

Birth Records

Birth records are another snap shot of the family and are an important source of family information. These records can be found in civil birth registers and in church baptismal registers. Birth records will list the name of the parents and this normally includes the maiden name of the mother. Knowing the maiden name of the mother is a critical need to finding her parents and extending her branch of your family tree. Some birth records also include the home address for the family and the occupation of the father.

The record that you find may be the original that was filed at the time of the event. It may be an amended record that was revised to reflect corrections or new information such as the addition of the given name for the child. It may also be a delayed birth record that was created to establish a legal birth record for an individual who was born before the registration of births was required. Delayed birth records are sometimes needed by people to legally establish the date of their birth. An example of an event causing this need would be when they applied for their social security card.

Birth records that were created in the 1900s are usually easy to find but birth records for individuals born prior to 1900 may be a challenge to find. This may be true because marriages and deaths were recorded by churches and civil offices before birth records were required. Most early birth records were recorded by the church that the parents attended but many of these records were lost when small churches disbanded as the population moved westward and the records were not posted to neighboring churches or to local governments.

When you find a birth record, go beyond the genealogical data listed. Expand your family history by including a picture of the home where the parents were living. Also list the occupation of the father if it was on the record. If the record is a baptismal record, list who the godparents were, who performed the baptism and at what church. Include a picture of the church if possible. Also look for newspaper birth announcements that may contain more information.

More Information

*Sample 1892 Catholic Church Baptism Register in Latin
listing the names of the parents and the godparents*

Nomen Familiæ.	A.D. Die Mensis.	REGISTRUM BAPTISMORUM.	Observanda.
Franciscus Wolski 824	13. Novem 1892	Ego infrascriptus baptizavi Franciscum natum Die 6. Novembris A. D. 1892 ex Antonio Wolski ex loco Chicago et Anastasia Wenckowska ex loco Chicago Patrini fuerunt Adalbertus Wenckowski Apolonia Wenckowska Adolphus Snigurski	

Registrum Baptizatorum in Ecclesia _____ Diœcesis _____ 209

Birth registers are normally large ledge type books with a left-hand page and a right hand page. Be sure to copy and view both pages. The left page normally lists the date of birth, the name of the infant and the town of birth. The right hand page lists the name of the parents, their occupation and their place of residence.

1894 Michigan County Birth Register – Left page

1894 Michigan County Birth Register – Right page

More Information

Sample 1892 Illinois birth Certificate
Listing name of infant, place of birth,
names of parents and the occupation of father

1920s Birth certificate listing name of infant, place of birth,
names of parents, birthplace of parents and occupation of parents

Marriage Records

Churches and governments often kept marriage records before they began documenting births and deaths. If the ceremony was performed in a church, the event may have been recorded in both the civil registers and the church registers and both records should be reviewed because each may list different information. Remember to search for the marriage records for their siblings and cousins especially if they were born in the "old country."

Marriage records can contain important genealogical information. The records always will list the date of the ceremony and the names of the bride and groom. If you are lucky you may find the ages of the bride and groom, where they were born, the names of the parents, the name of the church, the name of who performed the marriage and the names of the witnesses. Since the bride and groom are there to give the information, the information should be accurate although spelling errors may occur. I also try to include a picture of the church or county court building where ceremony was performed.

1915 Marriage License that lists the names of the bride and groom,
the date of the marriage and the name of who performed the ceremony.
Compare this to marriage application shown on the next page.

More Information

1915 Marriage application the lists the names of the bride and Groom, their ages, their birthplaces, the names of their parents the name of the priest who performed the marriage and the names of the witnesses.

No. 25109

Marriage License
MINOR

Mr. Erwin J. Szabados

WITH

M. Elizabeth J. Takacs

Issued _____ 19___

Married _____ 19___

Filed _____ 19___

FILED MAY 15 1915
P. A. Guthrie
County Clerk, McLean County, Ill.

Registered _____ FILED MAY 16 1915 _19_

Marriage Register P. A. Guthrie
COUNTY CLERK, McLEAN COUNTY, ILL.

ILLINOIS STATE BOARD OF HEALTH

This return is to be carefully filled out and returned with the Marriage License. This return does not take the place of the Certificate which comes attached to the License, but is IN ADDITION THERETO.

Return of a Marriage to County Clerk.

1. Full name of GROOM Erwin J. Szabados
2. Place of residence Bloomington Ill
3. Occupation Machinist
4. Age next birthday 21 years. Color White Race
5. Place of birth Paukotta Hungary
6. Father's name Martin Szabados
7. Mother's maiden name Josephine Szente
8. Number of groom's marriage first
9. Full name of BRIDE Elisabeth J. Tackacs
    Maiden name if a widow _____
10. Place of residence Bloomington Ill
11. Age next birthday 18 years. Color White Race
12. Place of birth Erdohegy Hungary
13. Father's name Georg Tackacs
14. Mother's maiden name Elisabeth Yambor
15. Number of bride's marriage first
16. Married at Bloomington in the County of McLean and State of Illinois, the 12th day of May 19 15
17. Witnesses to marriage Stephan Bettisch & Lena Bettisch

N. B.—At Nos. 8 and 15 state whether 1st, 2d, 3d, 4th, &c., marriage of each. At 17 give name of subscribing witnesses to the Marriage Certificate. If no subscribing witnesses, give names of two persons who witnessed the ceremony.

Bloomington Ill May 12 1915

We hereby certify that the information above given is correct to the best of our knowledge and belief.

Erwin J. Szabados (Groom.)
Elizabeth Takacs (Bride.)

I hereby certify that the above is a correct return of a Marriage solemnized by me.

Rev Guido Stallo

Dated at Bloomington Ill this 12th day of May 12th 1915

Writing Your Family History

1906 Catholic Church Marriage register that lists the date, the names of the bride and groom, where they lived, their birthplace, the occupation of the groom, the names and birthplaces of their parents, the name of the celebrant and the names of the witnesses

1904 Catholic Church Marriage register that lists the date, the names of the bride and groom, the name of the celebrant and the names of the witnesses

More Information

Immigration - Passenger lists

The story of the arrival in America of your ancestors was an important event for your family. Their arrival and the arrival of the many immigrants that came before and after them are a large part of American history. Most U.S. citizens are descendants of immigrants. Did your immigrant ancestor work in the steel mills, packing house, the railroads or one of the many factories. Whatever job your immigrant ancestors had after their arrival in America, they contributed to the tremendous growth of this new country.

Passenger manifests listing our ancestors are the first documents that help describe their arrival and establish their roots in America. Finding their passenger manifest is important because it gives us a picture of when and where they left, when and where they arrived, to whom and where they were going in the United States. Also, were they traveling alone, with their family, with relatives or with friends?

The U.S. Customs Service has been recording the names of passengers arriving in America aboard ships since 1798. Most of the early shipping papers were mainly baggage lists or cargo manifests, but many of these lists also show the names of passengers. Many of these records are missing because there was no uniform national policy that covered the handling of the ship manifests until 1819. The surviving passenger lists from U.S. ports are now stored at the National Archives and most of them have been microfilmed, digitized, and indexed.

The Steerage Act of 1819 required the captain or master of all ships arriving in America to deliver a passenger manifest to a federal official. This was the first time the federal government required the documentation of the arrival of immigrants. For arrivals prior to the steerage act, genealogists have to rely on finding lists generated for the ships' logs. Early formats for the passenger manifest that were used after the Steerage Act listed the passenger's name, age, gender, occupation, what country they left and what country was their destination.

After 1893, formats were gradually expanded and in late 1907 they became two pages. This larger format listed marital status, last residence, the ability to read or write, final destination in the U.S., name of friend or relative in the U.S., the name of relative where they left, mother tongue, if they had been in the U.S. prior, physical description and birthplace.

Formats for Passenger manifests after 1900 will list one to four town names depending on the year of immigration. I have found that the town names listed have been very helpful in my research but the spelling of the names usually have problems. Most immigrants were illiterate so their information was usually entered on the document phonetically. This led to many misspellings but remembering that the names were written phonetically should still prove helpful.

Passenger manifests used in the early 1900s are exciting to view because they list many interesting facts that gives us great insights about our immirant ancestors. Information listed on the passenger manifests grew as officials became concerned with the quality of the immigrant entering the United States. The manifests started with a basic list of the immigrants with their ages, occupatins and country of origin. Destinatons, last residence, birthplaces and who and where they left were added in later stages. Changes in immigration laws in 1906 and 1907 added questions about the amount of money the immigrant had, if they had been in the U.S. previously and who had paid for the passage. This format also inclused their height, color of hair, color of their eyes, complexion and listed any identfying marks.

Writing Your Family History

Portion of 1909 passenger manifest listing occupation, nationality, race, last residence, who and where they left & destination (columns 6,7,8,9,10,11,12)

Portion of 1909 passenger manifest with questions on previous travel, moneyes, destination and health (columns 14, 15, 16, 17, 18, 19, 20, 21, 22 & 23)

Portion of 1909 passenger manifest listing description of immigrant (columns 25, 26, 27 & 28)

More Information

The census records for 1900, 1910, 1920 and 1930 can be a source to give you clues as when your ancestors arrived. These census records listed the year of arrival and their naturalization status. The years listed on each census record may vary but using a range of years will still help you narrow your search.

The myth of name changes

Many family oral histories believe that family names were changed when immigrants entered America. This is a myth. Names on passenger manifests were based on official documents presented by the immigrant to the ship line at the time of boarding. It would be illegal to change their names. Also, immigration stations were staffed with large numbers of translators to help insure the information that was given by the immigrants was recorded accurately. If families changed the spelling of their surnames they did it after arrival and this was usually due to daily problems in its use and to make it easier for the people around them to pronounce their name.

Name variations and spelling

Some instances of variations in names found on passenger manifests may be have been caused when the ship's purser did not use the immigrant's documents as prescribed. Instead he wrote the name on the manifest from questions he asked the immigrant. Many immigrants could not read and this may have caused the mis-spelling of names. Some immigrants may have been able to recognize their name written in the Cyrillic alphabet or in Hebrew but could not recognize that the purser wrote the name phonetically in the Latin alphabet.

Remembering that your ancestor's name may be listed on the passenger manifest as a variant should help you find your ancestor faster. Use the correct spelling first and if your ancestor is not found, use name variations and wild cards. First names are important in your search and many variants of given names could be used. Sometimes it is best to use a portion of the given name with wild cards to reduce the problem with the given name variants. I have found two books that have useful lists of given name variants - _Foreign Variations and Diminutives of English Names_ by U.S. Department of Justice and _First Names of the Polish Commonwealth: Origins & Meanings_ by William F. Hoffman. Note that William Hoffman's book will list given names in more languages than Polish. Another problem with given names was caused when the immigrant preferred to use their middle name but their exit documents required the purser to list their first name on the passenger manifest.

Immigration - Naturalization papers

The naturalization papers are the last step for your ancestors in establishing your roots in America. The papers will verify that your ancestor became a U.S. citizen and the information found on the papers will vary depending when they were done. Early papers had only the country they left, the date that citizenship was granted and where it was granted. Later documents included many more details such as birthplace, date of birth, date of arrival, name, birth information and arrival information for their spouse and children.

The original naturalization act was passed in 1790 and stipulated that anyone who wanted to become a citizen of the United States must be a free white person who "behaved as a man of good moral character.

The steps to citizenship included:
1. Residence in the United States for at least two years
2. Residence in the state where they were applying for at least one year
3. Two witnesses must attest to the person's moral character and residency

Congress passed another Naturalization Act in 1795 that extended the residency requirement from two years to five years. The petitions were filed in county, territorial, state or federal courts. Knowing which court that was available is an important clue as to where to look for your ancestor's petition.

The Naturalization Petition is another document that describes the arrival of your ancestors and their early life in their new country. However, remember that naturalization was considered a privilege and not a requirement. The primary motivation for naturalization was the right to vote. Many immigrants did not go through the naturalization process. Some immigrants arrived with the intention of earning enough money to go back to their home country and buy land. Some of these ended up staying in the U.S. and never returning home. Census records can be used to determine if the immigrant was naturalized. 1890 was the first year individuals were asked if they were naturalized. On the census records, "AL" was listed for non-naturalized immigrants, "PA" was listed if they had submitted their declaration of intention and "NA" was listed if they have been naturalized.

Over the years, naturalization laws changed numerous times, but generally speaking the process required a Declaration of Intention and a Petition to be filed to become a citizen. Naturalization forms prior to 1906 included country of original, date of naturalization and the court where they were naturalized and usually did not include where they born or any other genealogical information.

Petitions submitted prior to 1906 did not require a town name. The pre-1906 petition usually listed only the country of birth.

After 1906, the certificate of arrival was created during the naturalization process.

Naturalization petitions submitted after 1906 will list the applicant's birth date, birthplace, date of arrival, place of arrival and the name of the ship. If they are married the petition will also list this information for their spouse and any children at the time of the petition. The birthplace listed could be the actual birthplace but may also be where your ancestor was baptized. Either name will be an accurate name to direct you to where to look for the records of your ancestor in the "old country". Note that there may still be variations in how the name is written if the immigrant was not literate and the person filling out the form wrote the name phonetically. You will still need to find more names that will indicate what area the birthplace is located but you will have a very accurate piece to your puzzle.

The Petition is the document that will list the most valuable information but the other documents may also add information to your family history.

Pre-1906 Naturalization Petition

More Information

1919 Naturalization petition (top half)

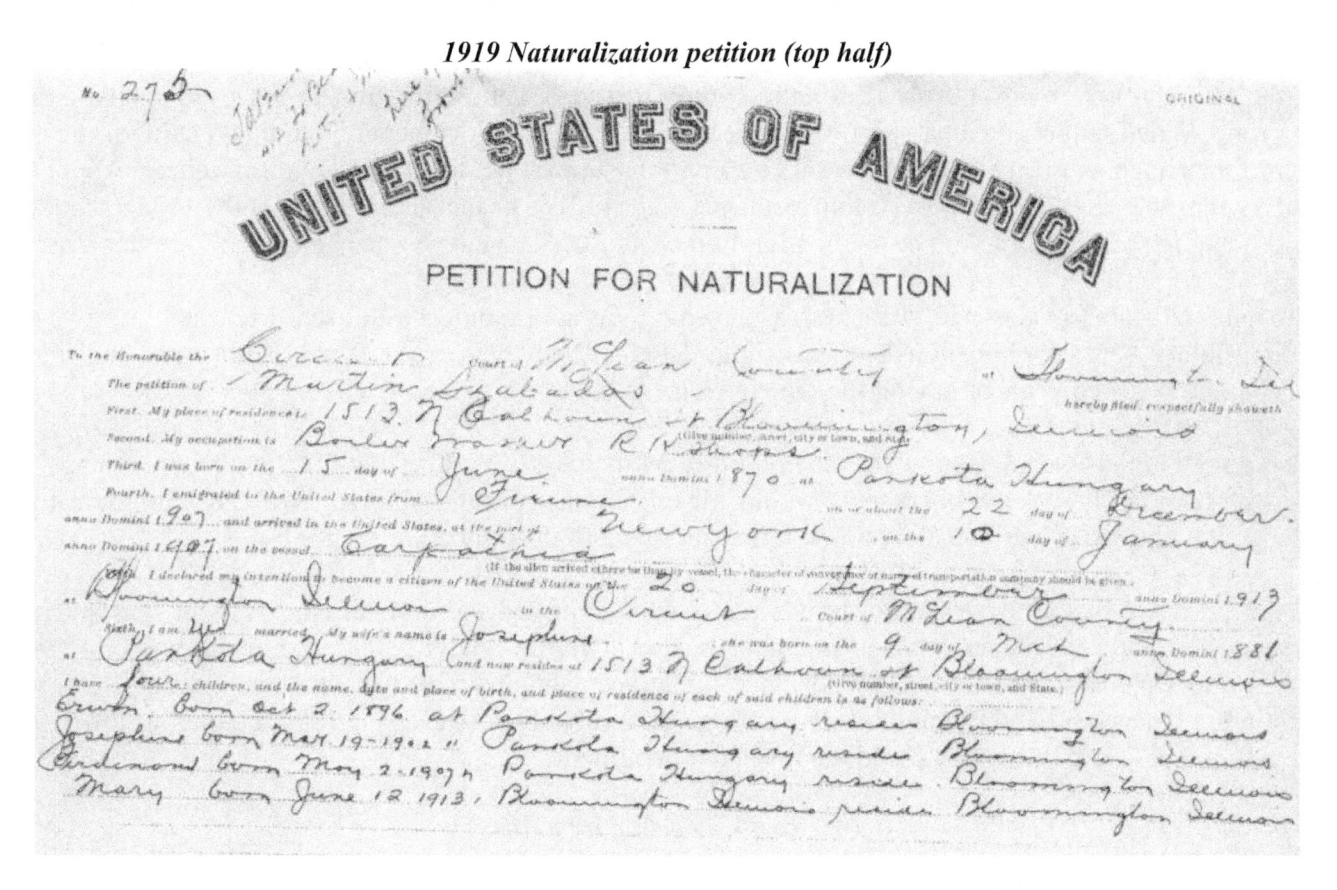

Below is the naturalization petition for my grandmother. It lists her birthplace as Andrejowo, Poland. There are a number of towns in Poland with this name so this entry only serves as one clue and other names are needed to find the exact location.

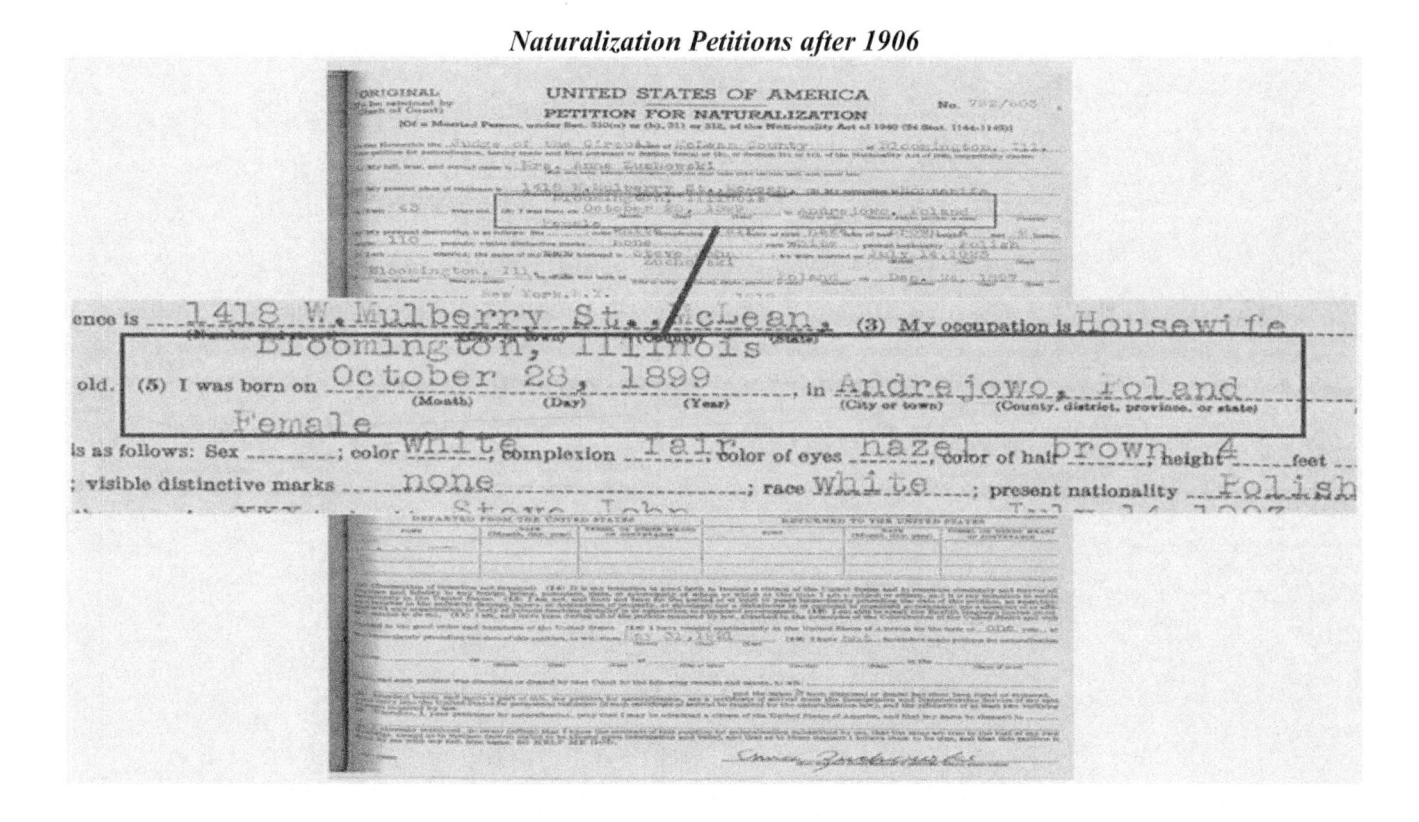

Naturalization Petitions after 1906

Other immigration documents - Exit Visas

In the late 1800s in many European countries, men had to obtain permission to leave their villages and emigrate. When requesting a passport, they had to submit several documents including a copy of the birth record, marriage, evidence of residence and occupation, supporting documents, and references. Applicants had to sign that they would waive their residence right to live in the village. If not, the village could be held liable for paying for return costs if emigration was refused or the people came back for other reasons.

The age and status of the man was one reason why emigration could be refused. Men had to prove that their military service obligation had been completed before they could leave. Sometimes this meant serving the required years or paying for someone else to take their place.

Also note that these legal documents were required by the passenger lines before passage could be sold to the immigrant. These legal documents would make it impossible for the name of the immigrant to be changed by the passenger line clerk or the immigration clerk in America.

The only source that I have found for Exit Visas of our immigrant ancestors are the desk drawers and shoe boxes filled with old documents and pictures. Ask your living relatives if they have seen any of these boxes and especially seek out descendants of relatives who may have been the caregivers for your immigrant ancestors before they died. The care givers probably sorted through the belongings after their ancestors died – hopefully they saved the treasured documents.

1876 Exit Visa listing from Austria

More Information

Military Records

Family oral history may give you hints that a family member served in the military. Military records for your ancestor can help you find evidence of military or patriotic service, give birth information, list relatives such as a parent or a sibling and list a residence at the time of military registration, enlistment, service or pension

A 1973 fire at the National Personnel Records Center in Saint Louis destroyed a significant portion of military service records for veterans who served in WW I through to the 1960s. Army records were the worst hit with roughly 85 percent lost. Note that prior to WW II, Air Force personnel were part of the Army Air Corps and thus were included in many of the records that were lost. Navy personnel records were generally not affected by the fire.

National Archives personnel are attempting to create new individual files for Army personnel from documents that were stored in files at other locations. These are not duplicate copies but other forms and papers that list information about individual military personnel. This requires searching all military files that were not in the St Louis Records Center at the time of the fire and trying to find documents that pertain to individuals and then placing copies of these documents in new files for the individuals. This will not replace all of the facts contained in the files that were burned but hopefully they will capture some facts of the service of personnel that were affected by the fire.

There are no duplicate records but there are many resources that can be searched to possibly find information about your ancestor. One place to start is Jennifer Holik's new web page WW II Toolbox at http://jenniferholik.com/world-war-ii-toolbox.html. Information on this web page includes many resources that can help you with research WWII military service. Look for resources may include your ancestor or may only give you general information about their service.

If you can obtain your ancestor's military service records, you will gain a treasury of facts to add to your family history. Other examples of some of the useful military records that I found are World I and World War II draft registrations which list the date of birth and birthplace of the applicants. Other useful sources that may be available are Civil War and Revolutionary War pension documents and discharge papers which list the date, place of birth, many additional facts such as the name of their spouse and children, the unit they serve with in the war and some describe the actions that they fought in.

Portion of a page from my grandfather's military service papers listing his rank and where he was assigned.

Writing Your Family History

The following are examples WW I and WW II draft registration cards:

WW I draft registration – note that it lists his birthplace

	REGISTRATION CARD
1	Name: Anthony Chmielewski Age: 24
2	Home address: 22 Wood St., Terryville Conn
3	Date of birth:
4	Are you (1) a natural-born citizen, (2) a naturalized citizen, (3) an alien, (4) or have you declared your — An Alien
5	Where were you born? Gorski (Town) Poland (State) Russia (Nation)
6	If not a citizen, of what country are you a citizen or subject? Russia
7	What is your present trade, occupation, or office? Lockmaker 15
8	By whom employed? Eagle Lock Co. Where employed? Terryville Conn.
9	Have you a father, mother, wife, child under 12, or a sister or brother under 12, solely dependent on you for support (specify which)? Wife and 2 Children
10	Married or single (which)? Married Race (specify which)? Caucasian
11	What military service have you had? Rank No branch ___ years ___ Nation or State ___
12	Do you claim exemption from draft (specify grounds)? Yes Wife 2 Children

Birthplace in Russia (pointing to field 5)

I affirm that I have verified above answers and that they are true.

Anthony Chmielewski (Signature or mark)

More Information

WW II draft registration – note that it lists his birthplace

REGISTRATION CARD—(Men born on or after April 28, 1877 and on or before February 16, 1897)

Serial Number	1. Name (Print)	Order Number
U 1542	John Chmielewski	

2. Place of Residence (Print): 45 Ash St., Jersey City, Hudson, N.J.

[THE PLACE OF RESIDENCE GIVEN ON THE LINE ABOVE WILL DETERMINE LOCAL BOARD JURISDICTION; LINE 2 OF REGISTRATION CERTIFICATE WILL BE IDENTICAL]

3. Mailing Address: Same

4. Telephone: None

5. Age in Years: 47
   Date of Birth: 12-24-1894

6. Place of Birth: Czuzuw, Poland

7. Name and Address of Person Who Will Always Know Your Address: Mrs. Stella Chmielewski - 45 Ash St.

8. Employer's Name and Address: Lehigh Valley Railroad

9. Place of Employment or Business: Washington St., Jersey City, Hudson, N.J.

I Affirm That I Have Verified Above Answers and That They Are True.

John Chmielewski (Registrant's signature)

D. S. S. Form 1 (Revised 4-1-42) (over)

Writing Your Family History

Next is the Civil War discharge paper for Silas Howard. This document was passed down through four generations and is an example of the importance of documents like this because it is the only document that lists when and where he was born.

More Information

Employment/Retirement Records

Due to privacy issues, employment records for your ancestor will be difficult to obtain from their employer. Their employers will probably acknowledge the years that your ancestor was employed but refuse to release any individual information. This is unfortunate because the employment application will have many personal facts of your ancestor such as birthdates, birthplace, education and previous employment.

What employment records are available?
The answer to this question is "not many" and they are hard to find. The largest groups of employment records that I have found are for railroad employees and the next few pages will discuss these records.

Retirement papers for all railroad employees
I have found that the retirement pension files for railroad employees are available from the Railroad Retirement Board (RRB). Legislation was enacted in 1934, 1935, and 1937 to establish a railroad retirement system. RRB administers the pensions of all railroad employees from all companies and their records are separate from the social security program that was legislated in 1935. Their files include not only the employee's pension applications but also numerous papers concerning service dates and in some case the amount of pay. Marriage and insurance information may also be included.

Below is a copy of a page from my grandfather's railroad retirement file that lists his birthplace.

If your ancestor worked for the railroad but did not receive a pension, the Railroad Retirement Board will not have any file on them. You will need to search historical archives to find these records if they exist.

Writing Your Family History

Another page from my grandfather's railroad retirement papers.
This lists his early work earnings for Social Security Verification

More Railroad Employment Records

Pullman-Standard was the leading producer of railroad passenger cars in the early 1900s. The company also played a leading role as an arsenal during WW I and WW II when it produced freight cars, tanks, and munitions for America's war efforts during both World Wars. Thousands of employees from Northwest Indiana and Chicago contributed to the success of Pullman-Standard at their Hammond, Michigan City, and Chicago locations. Since employees routinely transferred within the Pullman-Standard plants located in Indiana and Illinois, information on a particular employee may be scattered between sources in Indiana and in Illinois

I found that the South Suburban Genealogical Society (SSGS) in Crestwood, Illinois was able to save the personnel files for the employees from the now closed Pullman Standard Car Works plant in Chicago,

More Information

Illinois. In 1982, the Society somehow was able to save employment files that cover the period from about 1900 through World War II and account for approximately 152,000 Pullman employees. Prior to South Suburban taking possession of the records, they had been stored in a wood kiln in Hammond, Indiana. In January of 1983, the SSGS started alphabetizing more than a million Pullman employment documents (they were previously kept in numerical order). It took six years and 2,560 volunteer hours to clean, re-box, and index this massive collection. The files may include many personal papers such as birth certificates. The Pullman collection is not open to the public. Research is done only by authorized volunteers. SSGS staff will search the Pullman files at no charge to find if your ancestor is in the records but there is a fee if you order a copy of the file. The efforts of the South Suburban Genealogical Society are just one example of what files may be available.

The Calumet Regional Archives holds the employee records for the Pullman Car Works that were in Hammond, Indiana. These records have been cataloged by volunteers from the Northwest Indiana Genealogical Society and the index can be searched on the NWIGS website using their Online Archives and/or Research Resources page at: http://www.rootsweb.ancestry.com/~innwigs/
More Pullman employee records can be found at the Newberry Library in Chicago which has the files for the Pullman car service employees (such as Porters, etc).

Many railroad historical societies have been able to save railroad employment records. The Chicago and Northwestern Historical Society have many employee records that contain great genealogy information. Unfortunately, many records for other railroads were destroyed as railroads merged or went out of business. Some records were also destroyed just because they were old and the railroad did not see any value in keeping records for the deceased. To find the records that have been saved you will have to know for which railroad your ancestor worked. A useful source for this information is books called "The Official Railroad Guide." These books were published every 3 months and listed the schedule for every train in all towns in the United States. It also contained an index that listed all towns in alphabetical order that had a train station. To find which railroad company your ancestor worked for, find one of these guides for the appropriate time period and look for the town where your ancestor lived. Next, the page for the town will name of the railroad that serviced the town. Your should be able to find a copy of the Official Railroad Guide at most railroad historical groups, some state libraries, some university libraries and large genealogy libraries.

Employment records for other companies
More employment records from defunct companies may have been saved by local genealogy or historical groups. As an example, I found the employee cards from the Gary Screw and Bolt Company listed on the NWIGS web site. Most records for defunct companies were destroyed when their offices were cleared out. However, try contacting local societies where your ancestor worked to see if they have any employment records for local companies - you may find a treasure. Note this is not true for companies that were merged or purchased since the files of the old company would have been merged into the new company.

Most employments records may not be available due to privacy concerns and due to the fact that older files would be stored in archives and not available for public viewing. The Railroad Retirement Board does offer copies of the files for their retirees for a search fee. Also some genealogy societies and libraries have been able to save the personnel files for some defunct companies and these would be available for genealogical research.

Death Records

Death records such as death certificates and obituaries may list some important family information for the researcher. I have seen listed the age of the deceased, their place of residence, place of death, name of their spouse, name of their parents and their place of birth. However this information is not listed on all the documents that I found. We should also be concerned with the accuracy of the information on these documents because it may have been provided by someone who may have not known the facts. Many times the record only lists the country of birth and not the town or many times the birth place is listed as "unknown." The information also may be wrong because the information was given by someone who did not know or remember the correct information. If the death certificate or obituary lists a birthplace, use it as a place name to include on your list of clues but remember that it may be the least accurate.

In order to judge the accuracy of the information on death records, review the death certificate for the name of the informant. The information may be accurate if the informant was also born in the same birth place. If the informant was one of the children who were born after immigration, the information should be used carefully and the place name given may be a phonetic spelling. Below is an example of a death certificate. Most of the information is accurate but the birthplace lists only the country.

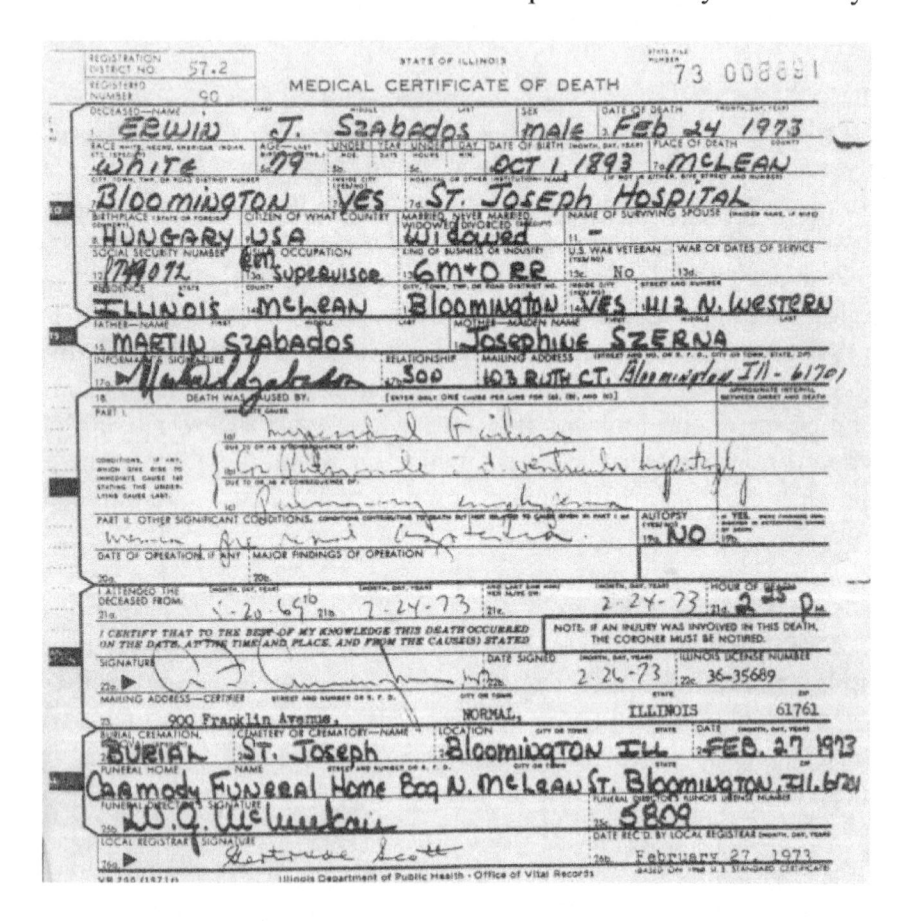

Many obituaries give only the name of the person who died, the names of their spouse and children and other surviving members of his family. Occasionally some families give many more details. A more detailed obituary is a good source for information about a person. It gives the name of the deceased and the date of death, ate of burial and the name of the cemetery. It may also contain information such as the birth date, place of birth, marriage date, names of parents and spouse, children, occupation, education, and the location of living family members at the time the obituary was written. Obituaries that list the names of children can also be used to track down the living descendants and possibly find more documents and information.

More Information

County Records
County records of interest to us were generated in both the county offices and the courtroom and can yield valuable family history information. Earlier we discussed how births, marriages and deaths were recorded by county officials and many naturalization papers were filed in the county courts. County records that we may also find are land records and probate records for your ancestors. Other court records that could list your ancestors are civil trials, criminal trials and jury rosters.

Land records
There are usually two land or deed records for each place your ancestor owned. One was when they purchased the property and the other was when they sold it. Some counties may keep all transactions for the property on one ledger so the ownership of the property can be tracked while it is in existence. These records are found in the county recorder's office. Tax records will also be available in the county assessor's office. These documents will help you find the location of each property that your ancestor owned and will give you valuable information about their history such as the price they paid for the property, any improvements that affected the taxes, when was the property built and how much your ancestor received when they sold the property.

Another important document that would be useful in your genealogical research would be a tract map for the county. This normally indicates the owner of each section of land and should show you the location of your ancestors land if they were a farmer. Historical tract maps may be available from the local county historical society and possibly at the recorder's office.

Portion of the 1892 Plat of Swan River Township, Morrison County, Minnesota
note that each section is labeled with the name of the owner

Wills & Probate Records

Probate records are court records dealing with the distribution of a person's estate after death. They were recorded much earlier in history than birth, marriage, and death registration. Probate records are very useful for family history research because they recorded the death date, names of heirs, family members, guardians, relationships, residences and inventories of the estate. Also remember that probate records were not created for every person who died.

The illustration on the right is an example of an affidavit that was used to probate the estate of a farmer and transfer his property to his wife. The Affidavit was given by two of the sons of a deceased farmer.

An inventory of the estate will give an idea of the worth of the deceased and it can also indicate the names of people around the deceased by listing the people who owed him money or who he owed. It may also give clues as to his occupation.

1908 General Affidavit given by two sons of the deceased about the death

Below is an 1860 Probate record for Silas Howard that was submitted by his brother Calvin. It was important because it listed the parents of Calvin and Silas and six other brothers and sisters.

1860 Surrogate Petition by Calvin Howard

More Information

Other Court records

Your ancestors may also be found in court records if they served on a jury or were part of a civil or criminal action as a witness, defendant or plaintiff. Some of these records have been saved by historical societies. Occasionally early records may be listed in county histories but the county court houses are the main location where trial records are found. If your ancestor was a plaintiff or defendant, they may be listed in the register of cases for the court. If they were on a jury or a witness it will be challenging to find them. Before you start browsing through the case files for the many trials that may list your ancestor you should verify that they actually served on a jury or were a witness.

Another point to remember is that county boundaries changed and the old homestead may have actually been part of multiple counties over time. County records stayed with the original county. To find a county record you will need to know what county was in existence at the time the record was created.

Tax Records

There are three types of tax records that may help with genealogical research – poll taxes, real estate taxes and personal property taxes. Tax records are generate annually and will list basic personal information such as name, address, occupation, real estate owned, personal property owned and value of their property. The real genealogical value from tax records comes from tracking when your ancestor appears, when they disappear from the tax rolls and when males with the same surname appear next to them on the tax rolls or on a separate tax list for single men. This will allow you to determine when your ancestor move to a location, when their sons turned twenty-one and when they got married. You may be able to discover the birth, marriage or death year of your early ancestor when no other record may have survived.

Some counties list occupation as a category on the tax record to avoid confusion between two individuals with the same name. Also remember a father may pass his trade on to son.

Tracking annual tax rolls can be used to determine year of birth and year of marriage for young men. The legal age for owning land was 21 years. A male who suddenly appears on the same assessment roll as your ancestor is probably a son who has just turned 21 and his birth year can be calculated. Some counties created a separate list for unmarried men. A young man coming of legal age would also be taxed on his personal property which was usually a horse or a cow. Once married, his name would leave the single man's list and suddenly appear on the regular list with other heads of families and this would give you the year of their marriage.

You can determine the year your ancestor arrived in the county by his first appearance on a tax record. Remember that early counties were formed by splitting up older counties. Make sure that you are looking in the correct county for the tax records for your ancestor. They may appear in both counties. First in the older county before the creation of the new county and then in the new county. Use the same logic to determine the year your ancestor left the county. If the records show enough detail, you may be able to track your ancestor across county and even state lines by matching occupation, livestock, or any unusual taxable items. Always use a series of years and *always* look in every township in the county. Townships like counties were also divided.

Obviously, a man will disappear from the tax lists when he dies. The death can be confirmed when his estate is still taxed awaiting probate.

In summary tax records can be used to find information when vital records do not exist. They can also list information such as migration, occupation and personal property that can give treasured details to the life of your ancestor.

County Histories

Writing county histories became popular in the late 1800s and early 1900s. Many town and county histories were produced for the American Centennial in 1876 or for the 100th anniversary of the founding of the county.

These histories included short biographical sketches of prominent citizens. If your ancestor was an early settler in a county, they may have been mentioned in one of these county histories and this can be a valuable resource for your family history. Local histories and old genealogies can be invaluable and usually are worth the extra effort it takes to track them down.

On the right is an example of a short biography for an ancestor that I found in "An Illustrated History of Union and Wallowa Counties" Oregon. This was written in 1902 when many of the early settlers or their children were alive and living in the area. Asher R Robinson in this example was alive and available to be interviewed for the details of his biography. This biography gave many details of his life that will not be found in any other documents. This information can also be used to search for other documents such as land records, passenger records, census records in unexpected locations and clues on other histories to review.

However, the biographical sketches contained in these books are usually referred to a "mug books" and the information found should be used with caution. Many genealogy researchers have compiled their family histories using erroneous data because they relied exclusively upon material that they found in these biographical sketches. Typically these books were published through a subscription with many of the subscribers having biographical sketches included in the book. A picture of the subscriber could be included for an extra fee. Biographies of rich and famous people were also included to help the publishers sell books to buyers who hadn't subscribed. The cost of a subscription varied by location and publisher and could have cost up to sixty or seventy dollars.

Exert for Asher Robinson from the County history – An Illustrated History of Union and Wallowa Counties

> On July 27, 1829, Asher R. was born to Asher and Betsy (Worden) Robinson, in Somerset county, Pennsylvania, whence seven years later he was removed by his parents to Michigan, where the father pre-empted eighty acres and built a home. The son assisted in tilling the farm and attended school until 1849; then his spirit was ready to take part in life's battle on his own account and he went to the famous pineries of the Peninsular state, operating there until he was twenty-seven years of age. In 1856 he started on the long and dangerous trip via Panama to the Pacific coast, landing in Sierra county, California, in due time, where he at once commenced to mine. Rather poor success attended his efforts in this line, and he turned toward the north, going to the Okanogan and Simjlikameen rivers, where he prospected for a time and then repaired to Walla Walla and operated a pack train to the mining camps of northern Idaho in partnership with Ed Payne. In October, 1862, he came to the Grande Ronde valley with his train, and at once took a government claim of one hundred and sixty acres, two miles from the present site of Cove. In stock raising and farming until 1885 he was occupied on this farm, adding more by purchase and going into partnership with Ed Payne. In 1885 he sold out and went into a livery stable in Cove, which he ran successfully for a time, and then retired from active business to enjoy the competence that his faithful and wise labor had provided for him.

The sketches generally contained details of the people's lives but always giving a positive picture. After all, these people were paying to be included and the publishers did want them to buy the book.

More Information

The mug book publishers may have tried to give the people represented in the biographies every opportunity to insure accuracy in the biographies and they believed that they were giving their readers a volume containing few errors of consequence. However, the subject of the sketch could edit out anything unflattering and add in whatever they wanted. Errors of omission are likely and factual errors were not uncommon.

Also, keep in mind that the person who was the subject of most of the biographical sketches had paid to have the biography written and this would encourage to have the sketch to highlight only the positive aspects of this person's life. It's also possible that stories and facts may have been exaggerated.

Information found in county, town and church histories varies greatly in depth and accuracy. One should always be careful about accepting anything and everything in print as 100 percent accurate. Information that is un-cited should be especially suspect. If the information was based on an interview, it is difficult to weigh the credibility of the source. Could the person be an eyewitness to an event or merely re-telling stories he or she had heard?

However, you should try to verify the facts listed in the county history. The accuracy of the history depends upon the bias and abilities of the author and the resources available to them. The histories were written using various levels of documentation such as tax records, court records, and minutes from county meetings, church histories and interviews with older residents. You need to take all of this into consideration when using a county history to "discover your ancestor's place in history."

Even with the shortcomings, county histories and biographies are great secondary sources for genealogists. They often list parents, siblings, children, spouses, and in-laws. Other information that may be found are stories of their migration and pictures of the individual. Information on births, marriages, death, and burial dates and locations. Since vital records were not usually kept until the late 1800s or early 1900s, information found in these biographies may be the only source. Other information often found includes occupations, religious and political affiliations, and societies in which the individual was a member. Also check to see if their siblings, cousins, or in-laws were featured in mug books and these may be an indirect way to glean more genealogical treasures.

Newspaper Articles

Newspapers can be excellent sources of family history. The family historian will find that newspapers of the late 19th and early 20th centuries can yield an abundance of personal news and social items for their ancestors. To expand your family history, go beyond announcements for births, weddings and deaths. You may think that your ancestors may not be important enough to be included in news articles but there are many stories of interest that may include ordinary people. Many editors of early newspapers felt free to express their opinions on any given subject, and to describe local scandals in detail. Local newspapers can show more insights of your ancestors through announcements of anniversaries, legal notices, letters to the editor, and social columns filled with local news of a more personal nature. This can provide a gold mine of information for your family history. No matter what size the newspaper is or what where it is located, newspapers can open a new window into the lives of your ancestors.

Examples of items that may be found are:
- News stories may list your ancestor being interviewed or as a participant. These include stories of fires, nature disasters, crimes and scandals. They may also appear in personal interest stories, in the minutes of the proceedings of meetings of local governing bodies or in the listings of candidates for upcoming elections. .
- Society news and local gossip - Most newspapers had a column for residents to submit local news that might be of interest to others. This would often include such tidbits such as birthday announcements, illnesses, job promotions, wedding announcements, visitors to the community, community events, contests, holiday celebrations; notices of residents who have moved to other locations; and other news of a more personal nature.
- Advertisements included listing for the sale of livestock, farm equipment, and even personal property. were often sold at public sales which might be found listed in small classified advertisements.
- Announcements that may be of interest for the genealogist would be those concerning insolvent debtors, forced land sales, professional services, runaway slaves, and missing relatives.
- Transfers of real estate can also be found in columns in most newspapers.
- Legal notices for such actions as proving of wills, land sales for payment of taxes, divorce proceedings, proving of heirs, sheriffs' sales and the settlement of estates needed to be done as a legal step in the proceedings.
- Unclaimed mail lists were needed by post offices in early settlements because of the movement of settlers westward. This was an attempt to find finds or relatives that knew where the recipient moved so the mail could be forwarded to them. This would identify when your ancestors mover to a new location.
- Church announcements included lists of new members, baptisms, confirmations, and other church news to local newspapers for publication.
- Military news were announcements about hometown boys who were serving in the military during both peacetime and wars. The news item may be about completing training, returning home on leave, about being wounded, missing in action, captured or killed.
- School news and activities would be a treasure piece of information for the family historian because it may include lists of students who made the honor roll, awards won by area students, school board minutes, school events, and detailed coverage of annual graduation ceremonies.

The online sources that I have used with success are Newspapers.com and GenealogyBank.com. I have found that the online resources at local libraries are useful. Many libraries also have films with the digital copies of their local newspapers for review. There are many more online newspaper resources available and I recommend browsing the "newspaper" category on Cindi's List at http://www.cyndislist.com. The advantage of the online resources is that you can search the digital images by your ancestor's name or topic.

Published Family Histories

You may be surprised to find someone may have published a book that covers one branch of your family history. My son-in-law has ancestors who arrived on the Mayflower and this gives me many details for these branches of his family. I have also found books that cover two other less prominent branches. These histories start with the story of the patriarch who immigrated to Colonial America and then lists many descendants and some of their stories.

Connecting to families can add a tremendous amount of information to your family history but caution should be used to verify that the information that you find in this type of published books. Many times you will find the information in these books are not cited but you can use the information found in these books as clues. Always verify the details and the relationships by using standard genealogical research and analysis processes. The family histories may not cite the sources but will give you clues on where to look for the documents.

One of the Books on family history that covers a branch of my son-in-laws' families

The Hinderliter / Hinterleitner Saga
A Journey in Time

by
Andrew F. Hinderliter
&
Walter L. Davis

CHAPTER FOUR – EVALUATING AND CITING SOURCES

As I began writing family histories, memories of my high school English teacher reviewing the rules for citing sources and footnotes came to mind. This was something that I did not enjoy but accepted the reasons for why it was necessary. When writing your family history, it is also important for you to cite your sources. For each specific fact that you note in your family history that is not common knowledge, you need to tell the reader where you got the information. Basically, you need to name the document that contains the information and who created the document. Citing the source of your information lends credence to your work and ensures your family members that your family history in not fiction. If you contradict a part of your family oral history, your family will be more likely to accept your version if they can see the document where you found your information. The document will confirm that what you state is closer to fact than the oral history that has been stretched by the many generations who passed it along.

This will briefly cover the methods and reasons for citing and evaluating your sources.

Citing your sources

A *source* is the record, document or oral history that contains the information you need. The citation describes who created the record and where it is stored. The citation shows the path from the source that you used as evidence to support your conclusions. To be effective, citations must be complete and consistent. Citations may be placed in a variety of locations in the document that is being created. It can be in parentheses within the text, it may be shown as footnotes at the bottom of each page or it may be endnotes which are the same as footnotes but at the end of a chapter or at the end of the work.

Genealogical researchers should be methodical especially when documenting their sources. It is important to list the information needed for the citation before you start reading the document and taking notes. The excitement of finally having the long sought document or microfilm in your hands may tempt you to begin looking for the information about that elusive ancestor but take the time to detail the source before you forget to do it.

The information you need to include for your citation is similar to the rules you used to write your term papers in high school. Citation for books should include author, title, publisher, place of publication and year of publication. For magazines, newsletters and journal articles, you should record the author, article title, periodical name, volume and issue and date of publication.

Books
Sample endnote for a basic book using the format: endnote number, author, title, subtitle, publisher, date, page

23. Stephen Szabados, Write Your Family History: Easy Steps to Organize, Save and Share, (Summerville, SC: KDP, 2014), 69

Genealogy sources such as microfilm and extracts should be cited with similar information but also includes the roll number and other identifying information.

FHL Films
Sample endnote for an archive film from the Family History Library using the format: Church, location, Record Series, Owner/Repository, Film ID, Film Repository, Film location

Parafja Andrzejewo (Ostrów Mazowiecka), Kopie ksiąg metrykalnych, 1808-1881, Kościół rzymsko-katolicki, FHL microfilm 810584; Family History Library, Salt Lake City, Utah. (Note some of the information is in Polish as found in the catalog)

Many books that are used in genealogy were printed in short runs and may be hard to find. It may be helpful that the citations for this type of publications should list the library, archive or online database where you find the information. Future researchers may wonder where you found this book and this may also be a helpful reminder to you at a later date.

If your information was never published, such as a letter, a diary, public records, a gravestone, a church record or even an email message, you should state who wrote it, what it is, where it is now and give enough information so someone unfamiliar with your research could find that document or object again. Add notes about the condition of the item or special circumstances that impact your evaluation and analysis of it.

Online resources should also be cited. Elizabeth Shown Mills has published a very helpful reference to follow to capture the information from the internet. It is a four page booklet - "Quick Sheet Citing Online Historical Resources." It should be available at most large genealogy libraries and can be purchased from Amazon.com.

Online sources:
There are various formats that list different information in various sequences. The format shown below lists the database where the record was found but the focus is on the document and the person rather than the NARA publication. The specific information that is listed in the citation can be used to find the record on Ancestry.com.

Sample endnote for a 1910 Federal census record:
1910 U.S. Census, McLean County, Illinois, population schedule, Bloomington, p. 30, enumeration district (ED) 89, sheet 15 B, dwelling 314, Martin Szabados; digital image, Ancestry.com (http://www.ancestry.com : accessed 5 January 2006).

The above rules may sound like a daunting task and seeing the footnotes at the bottom of the pages of your history may distract the reader. If this is a concern, standard rules suggest endnotes be used.

I have tried to simplify the process in my family histories. My method is to identify the document in the sentence in the narrative where I state the facts and then include a copy of the document in the book – usually after the section for the individual. The label above the document includes the citation the other required information and where I found the document. This method covers most of the rules for citing your sources and makes your history more readable for your family members. Please note that this method will not be accepted for scholarly works. If your intent is to publish your family history to the general public, you should follow the standard formats for citing your sources that are listed in published guides.

Evaluating and Citing Sources

Here is a sample document from one of my family histories:

Entry in narrative: "A death certificate has been found of a third child, an infant son, who was stillborn on October 28, 1935."

Document found behind narrative:

Death certificate for Zuchowski Infant – October 28, 1935
Source – Family History Library film #1753856, image #918
Found in index "Illinois Deaths and Stillbirths, 1916-1947"

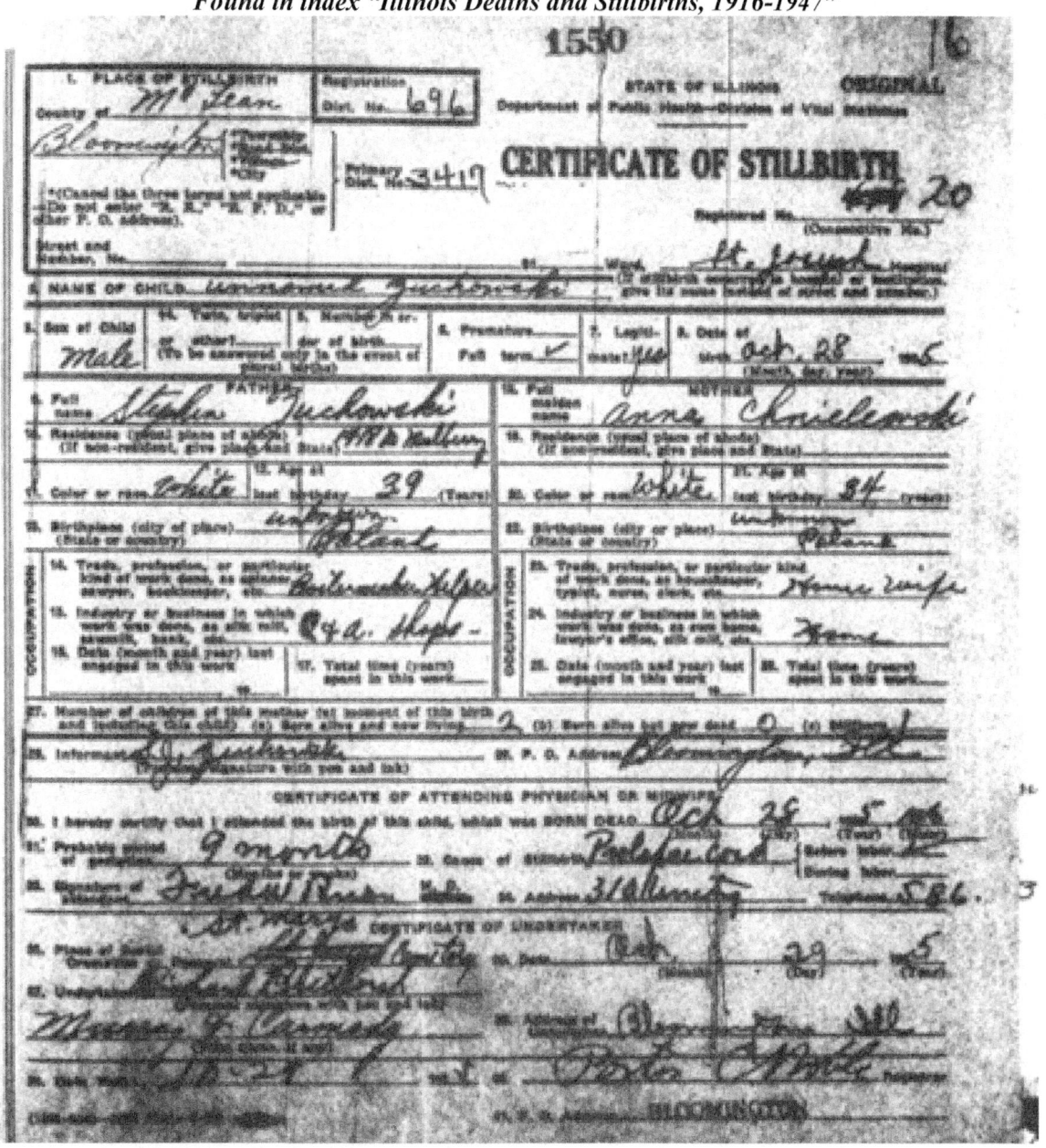

Passage from the family History "My Polish Ancestors" by Steve Szabados that reference to above document:
A death certificate has been found of a third child, an infant son, who was stillborn on October 28, 1935. The cause of death was prolapsed cord which means there was a problem with umbilical cord[23].

Sample endnote 23:
23. McLean County, Illinois death certificate no. 1550 (1935), infant Zuchowski; FHL microfilm no. 1,753,856, Family History Library, Salt Lake City, Utah.

You may hear arguments that keeping up with sources are time consuming and too much trouble. It isn't fun but without your source information you can't evaluate what you have found. You can't analyze and draw conclusions. And you can't pass along your information because at least one family member will ask, "But how do you know?"

Evaluating your Data
Genealogical Proof is the accumulation of acceptable evidence and consists of five conditions that a valid conclusion must meet:
- First is thorough and exhaustive research
- Second is having complete and accurate citations for the sources
- Third there must be a skilled analysis and correlation of data
- Fourth there must be resolution of any conflicts in the evidence
- Fifth there is a sound, coherent conclusion that details all the evidence, analyses and documentation.

You research should not be just collecting documents. As you find documents, you will need to continually analyze and interpret your information. The credibility of each piece of information needs to be determined. This is needed because some records may contain confusing and misleading information. It is important to state in your notes and summaries the source for all information that you find because this will help to determine the projected accuracy of your information as you analyze, interpret and formulate conclusions from your data. Knowing where your information came from will help evaluate its accuracy. As a beginner to genealogy, start now to carefully note where you get every piece of information. Cite your sources and analyze your evidence found in your data. The conclusions you use in your family history should represent the best possible scenario based on the evidence you have after a thorough and exhaustive search.

There are three types of conclusions that you will encounter when analyzing your information:
- First is a Hypothesis which is a proposition based on an analysis of the evidence that has been found thus far.
- Next is a Theory which is a tentative conclusion reached after a hypothesis has been extensively researched but the evidence is still short of being a proof.
- Finally is a Proof which is a conclusion based on the sum of the evidence that supports a valid assertion or deduction

Your search for evidence should go beyond the specific person. Research should be done on their family, friends and acquaintances. This should also include the place where the person lived. Research the counties and towns surrounding each place the person lived. You should also research not only the ancestor's entire life, but the lives of their parents, children, grandchildren, and so on, as needed.

Evaluating and Citing Sources

After finding documents, you now have to analyze and evaluate them for accuracy and relevance. The first evaluation to make is whether the record pertains to the person or family being searched. For example, the christening record of a person with the right name about the right time may be your ancestor but if they have a common name the record may be a person with the same name and not your ancestor. Look for other details on the record that may point to your family.

Each category of records has to be evaluated differently. Some tend to be more accurate than others.
- *Original sources* are the originally created documents. They are not a typed transcription or index. Original sources were created close to the time of the events they record. Even a source recorded close to the time of the event may have errors because the recorder may have made a mistake. An example of an original source is a birth recorded with the county.

Copy of original Birth Certificate

Writing Your Family History

- ***Derivative sources*** tend to be easier to use. Examples of a derivative source are a typed transcription and an index. They represent a reiteration of information from an original source. The author may not have had enough information to adequately interpret the other sources. On the other hand, the compiler may have known of errors in the other sources and corrected or explained them in the compilation. An example of a derivative source is an extract of a birth record provided by a county clerk. A birth index is another example of a derivative source. When a derivative source is encountered, every effort should be made to find a copy of the original source.

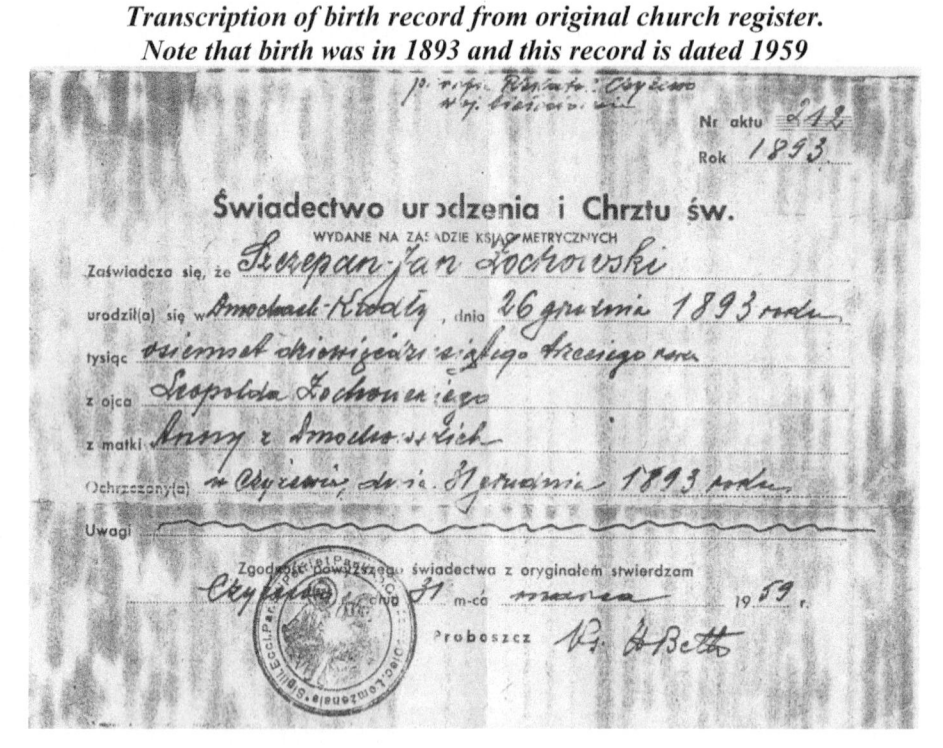

*Transcription of birth record from original church register.
Note that birth was in 1893 and this record is dated 1959*

- Note that photographic copies, including microfilm, microfiche, digital, and photocopies are virtually as good as the actual document, although they may sometimes be hard to read. Most of these are considered original sources.
- An original source *usually* carries more weight than a derivative source.

The nature of the information is also a key factor when evaluating its accuracy. Information is classified as primary or secondary based on who gave the information.

Primary Information was provided by someone who witnessed an event. The information was supplied by someone closely associated with the event. For example, a mother gives the birth date of her child. Primary information is usually found in original records but not all information in an original record is "primary." For example, a death record usually contains primary information about the death, but the birth information depends on who gave the information. If the parents or midwife gave the birth information then the information is primary. .

Secondary Information was provided by someone who heard information about the event but did not witness it. Secondary information is hearsay. For example, a son gives the birth date of his father. The further removed the informant is from the event or situation, the more suspect it becomes.

Evaluating and Citing Sources

Primary information *usually* carries more weight than secondary information. If the information does not come from a primary source, it may be suspect and should be verified. Secondary information may be correct but it needs to be verified. Multiple sources should always be used to draw a conclusion. All available sources should be used to determine if a conclusion is reasonable. A date in a birth record should be compared to census data for a person and with their death certificate. The question should be asked, "Do all sources support the same birth date?" If not, look for reasonable explanations why they do not have the same date. Birth records could be wrong, even though it's an original source. However, the chance for error is increased with secondary information because the recorder is not familiar with the events and may have been given incorrect information in the past. The researcher needs to ask who recorded the information and how the recorder knew what happened. This will help determine if the information is primary or secondary. Sometimes you may need to use secondary information because it may be the only record available. It should make sense with all other evidence accumulated.

Other aspects of evaluating the record pertain to the type of evidence it contains:

Direct evidence is straightforward evidence such as a death certificate will list the date of death; a birth certificate will list the date and place of birth and the names of the parents. If this information is what was sought then this is direct evidence.

Indirect evidence supports a fact by inference such as a census record will list a person's age and by calculation will give you a year of birth. However, other pieces of evidence are needed to arrive at a conclusion.

Consistent facts state information that does not conflict with other facts

Each record and each piece of information in a record should be evaluated individually. Each has to be examined for evidence of bias, fraud, time lapses, memory, losses and any other factors that can affect reliability of the information. Proof of each fact is the result of a thorough research and documentation; information that has been accurately interpreted and carefully correlated; and a well-reasoned analysis. To prove a fact, you must collect evidence that confirms one view and excludes other reasonable possibilities. Absolute proof is seldom possible, but a sufficient degree of proof should be the goal of each researcher. Also, direct evidence can sometimes be incorrect and often cases are solved having only indirect evidence. The accumulation of evidence and the analysis and correlation should be used by the researcher to create a well-reasoned summary that leads to a reasonable conclusion.

The material included is a brief summary of major points to consider in citing your sources and evaluating your information. However, there are many more aspects of the analysis of information and documentation that has not been covered in this chapter. For a greater understanding, please refer to other books of on this subject. The book *Evidence Explained: Citing History Sources from Artifacts to Cyberspace* by Elizabeth Shown Mills is highly recommended. I also presented a few examples of citations using the formats found in her book but these are a very small sample compared to the numerous formats that are given in the book.

Recommend reference

Elizabeth Shown Mills' book *Evidence Explained: Citing History Sources from Artifacts to Cyberspace* offers more details on citing your genealogical sources.

CHAPTER FIVE – MORE ABOUT WRITING FAMILY HISTORY

I have found that ggenealogy is not just the collection of names and information. At first my summaries were a list of facts but I see stories coming out of the information that I was finding. My ancestors had been living human beings who interacted with the people around them. Each document was a snap shot of their lives and I found that each detail should be captured and analyzed. Try to envision how each fact might impact your family's lives. Summaries will help you compile this information but try to go beyond the list of facts. Interpret the information and use the summaries to tell the story of your family.

My focus in the early stages in writing my family history was the research and identifying the stories that my relatives, documents and pictures told. My focus was not writing the history. The summaries that were the basis for the history were written to help with my research and to help share the information with my family. As I connected with family members, groups of summaries were merged together to share information about their ancestors. Over time the merged groups of summaries were combined and organized in one large document that became the family history that was published and distributed to the family members. As you can see the family history came together almost by accident and this method put very little pressure on me to produce such an important document. There was a lot of work to do the research and keep the summaries updated but the final document seemed to emerge and cry out to be published. Also note that the summaries and documents could also stay in the ring binders and not be published. The ring binder will still be organized enough for someone in the future to pickup and continue your work. However, publishing your work gives the family more copies of your work and more chances that your work will survive and be available for someone to continue your work.

Tell a Story

I stated earlier that the lives of your ancestors were more than the facts, documents and pictures that you find. All of these are related and your family history should show their relationship. Below is an example of this as I interpret some of the information about my grandparents that I try to find the story of how they met and married. The following is an example of the importance of writing your family history as a collection of related stories and going beyond the list of facts.

How did my grandparents meet?
- They grew up 4 miles apart but they were 6 years apart in age.
- They went to different parish churches.
- My grandfather left Poland to go to Bloomington Illinois at age 19 when my grandmother was 13.
- My grandmother immigrated 10 years later to Camden New Jersey.
- My grandmother's destination was her brother who lived at 1231 Jackson Street in Camden New Jersey.
- My Grandfather had a cousin who lived at 1221 Thurman Street in Camden, New Jersey – four blocks away from my grandmother's brother.
- The brother and cousin grew up living in villages about one mile apart.
- The brother and cousin probably met at the Polish Social Club in their neighborhood in Camden.

- The brother probably said "I have a sister coming to stay with me. She needs to be married because I have a wife and six children and there isn't enough room. Also I want to return to Poland because we are a country again."
- The cousin – "I have a cousin in Illinois that has a good job and is looking for a wife. I will write and ask him to visit me."
- My grandparents were married in Bloomington two years later.

The Story of the Marriage

There is no oral history as to how Anna Chmielewski and Steve Zuchowski met. One possible explanation is that they met in Camden, New Jersey while Anna was staying with her brother Hipolit at 1231 Jackson St and Steve may have been visiting his cousin Alexander Dmochowski who lived at 1221 Thurman Street which was four blocks north from Hipolit's house. It is very probable that Hipolit and Alexander met at the Polish Social Club in their neighborhood in Camden and they became friends.

Over 900 miles between Camden, NJ & Bloomington, IL

Hipolit also wanted to return to Poland and this may have motivated him to find a husband for his sister Anna. Alex may have invited Steve to visit when he heard Hipolit needed a husband for his sister.

The marriage certificate for Steve and Anna listed that they were married in St Patrick's Church in Bloomington Illinois on July 14 1923. After the wedding, they lived at 1316 W Market Street where their first child Regina was born on May 19, 1924.

St Patrick's Church in Bloomington, Illinois circa 1910

John and Anna with the Wedding Party Joseph and Martha Zulz plus Bernadette Uszcienski

Identifying more stories

An example of searching for the story is found in the picture to the right. This was one of three pictures of the family that I found in my mom's photo album. I believe that they are of a Polish family who are relatives of my grandmother. They may have immigrated to southern Illinois after WW II. The family was probably one of the many families who fled Poland after the communist takeover of the Polish government.

Information on the back of the back of the picture indicates that this was taken at the first communion of one of the girls in May of 1950 in Rochester. I found a Rochester, Illinois a few miles east of Springfield, Illinois. The photo album included two other pictures of the family showing the children slightly older. Unfortunately we have lost track of them but finding them may add more stories to the family history about my grandmother's family.

When and where was this picture taken, what was the event and who are these people

Social History

Other important parts of the lives of your ancestors were the people and events surrounding them. This is social history which is defined as the study of ordinary people's everyday lives. Using social history accurately in the family histories that we write will require we see historical events as they affect the group collectively and not one person. We are all affected in some way by the history that is occurring around us. This was also true about the lives of your ancestors and should be an important part of your family history. We may want to think of our ancestors as unique individuals. However, they were usually part of groups that reacted to the economic and political pressures that surrounded them at that point in history. Researching the historical context in which your ancestors lived will add historical background that may help answer questions and explain behaviors. Common elements in the daily lives of your ancestors that can be researched to add to the understanding of their lives are residence, occupation, religion, local politics, local economy, family migration, military experiences and social status. Identifying and understanding the events may explain one or more of their actions. Including these events could add important insights for your ancestors' life and family history. Including the social history that surrounded your ancestor will help portray them as real people and not just names on a chart.

When adding social history as a background for your ancestors be sure to cite your sources and draw your conclusions after presenting evidence that leads to those conclusions. Be careful not to fictionalize their lives by forcing lives into events that they did not take part. Avoid inserting famous historical events that are not relevant to your family history.

Using timelines is a trick that I have used that has proven very helpful when tracking my ancestors and matching their movements to historical events.

Writing Your Family History

Examples that I have used in my research:
- My son-in-law has ancestors who were on the Mayflower. A brief description of the voyage and early settlement adds a lot of interest and helps describe the lives of his ancestors at this time in history. There are many books available that describes the Pilgrims and in many cases by name.
- Do you have ancestors that fought in the military? If you can identify the unit that they were assigned, you can list the battles where they fought. Unit histories are available online and at military museums. The museums will generally have more materials that will yield greater detail and numerous pictures. If you are lucky, you may find pictures that include your ancestor.
- If your ancestor moved, try to identify if there was a historical event surrounding this move. An example is the movement to California about 1850 possibly may be explained by the California Gold Rush. In some cases, Family oral history or family papers may point to the cause for such a move but a careful study of history is needed to match the time table of the moves to specific historical events.
- Look in land records to see if ancestors were "homesteaders." Census will point to the area to search in county land records and the Bureau of Land Management online index can also be helpful.
- Track your ancestors with timelines to identify if they were early settlers in the Midwest or were pioneers on the Oregon Trail. Early county histories may mention them as early settlers and may also be a source for biographical sketches. The county histories may also describe early activities of the settlers and give you insight as to the activities for your ancestors.
- I have also found books on immigration that gave some possible scenarios of the reasons for immigration and their early problems after they arrived in America. The books that I found described the lives in villages in the "old country" and offer reasons that would cause them to leave. The material also described the various problems immigrants might have encountered on their journey from village to the port of their departure. The process the immigrants followed for boarding the ships, the problems they endured during the voyage and the challenges of they faced upon arrival are also depicted in many books and articles. Finding this material and using them to visualize your ancestors will change how you view your immigrants.

Always ask why your ancestors moved or why they were in a certain area. The answers are usually the availability of jobs, the availability cheap land, or persecution for religious or political reasons. .Do the research to answer these questions and your ancestors will come alive in your family history. The next question should be "How did they find out about this?"

Here is an example of social history before I blended it with my family:

After WW I began the U.S. military instituted a massive buildup of men and equipment. By 1918, Ford Motor Company was expanding to meet the surge in the demand to produce military vehicles. During the period between 1915 and 1920, Ford's production doubled from 501,462 in 1915 to over one million cars in 1920.

Here is an example of the above social history that includes my grandfather and explains his move from central Illinois to Detroit in 1918:

By 1918, Erwin had joined <u>Ford Motor Company</u> as a machinist <u>when the Ford was expanding to meet the surge in its production. During the period between 1915 and 1920, Ford's production doubled from 501,462 in 1915 to over one million cars in 1920.</u>

Erwin's 1918 draft registration indicated that he was living in Detroit Michigan at 322 Humboldt and that he was working for Ford Motor Company as a machinist. Although he registered for the draft, he was not called to service in the military. <u>*Since Ford had military contracts for the war effort, Erwin may have been exempted from the draft if his job was considered critical to the war effort.*</u>

WW I draft registration for my grandfather

I have used many sources for the social history that I have added to my histories. The information that I used for the California Gold Rush and the Oregon Trail was found in general history books. The voyage of the Mayflower and the early days of the pilgrims were found in the many books that I found at my local library. I also used the internet to find various articles and books about various topics such as the lives of homesteaders, the journey that immigrants endured. Other sources that may give historical references that can be used in our histories may be found in letters and diaries, cookbooks and food histories, biographies, historical fiction, histories of urban ethnic neighborhoods and county histories.

Using social history to add historical background information to my family history brings more life to my ancestors. However, including too many historical details may shift the reader's attention away from my ancestors. As a general rule I try to add as much social history as I can but these events must affect the lives of my ancestors. A brief history of the railroad shops in Bloomington will help explain why my family was in Bloomington seeking jobs. However, explaining the workings of all of the various departments in the shops is overkill.

In writing my histories, I am constantly analyzing and correlating the information that I find in the historical documents. I am making speculations and inferences about this information and I try to make the reader aware about how I came to these conclusions. It is also very important to make it clear what is verifiable information and what is historical background.

Your Audience

Next, consider who will read your history. Your audience will determine your format. Formats that I have seen or used are:

- Direct ancestors – starting with parents or Grandparents using pedigree chart as a guide (the basic focus for most of us)
- Famous descendants of a famous ancestor. Books with this format are normally found in libraries or archives and I think they were usually produced as a book for sale to the general public. They include a detailed biography for the famous ancestor and then sections for the various descendants.
- Story of a single ancestor or event. This can be a great project for someone who feels closely attached to a specific ancestor who has a storied past or is known in family oral history for a significant achievement.

Direct ancestors

The group picture shown below includes members of my immediate family and my extended family. Writing a family history that includes all of their ancestors would be a huge task and be very hard to organize. My solution was to break this large project into many pieces using parents or grandparents as the points of separation. This allowed me to design the format of each history to the unique audiences and make each person in that audience feel that it was about their family. Distribution of each history was to the members of each audience and not to everyone in the group picture. An example of this thought process is that descendants of my wife's siblings would not be interested in my ancestors and the same would be true of my cousins' interest in my wife's side of the family.

Another aspect to consider is determining who should be the focal point. If the main group in the audience is siblings, then their parents should be the starting point for the family history. If the main audience is cousins, then grandparents would be the logical focal point. For second cousins, third cousins or more, the closest common ancestor makes the most sense. For my mother's family history, the audience is myself, my sister and our descendants and I started with my mother and then listed all of her ancestors. For my

More About Writing Family History

dad's family history first and second cousins were the audience and I started with the common great-grandparents and their ancestors. I then discussed each set of grandparents in separate sections. I needed to include first and second cousins in the audience because of the amount of information that I received from this large group. I then included research for the ancestors of their grandmother or grandfather who had married into the family. This was a thank you for their cooperation and it also made them feel that this was their family history. I included these extra branches as appendices at the end of the book and one of these sections was my grandmother. The next page shows the table of contents from this family history. As you can see, the further you go back to find the common ancestor to make the focal point, the more complicated the format will be and larger your audience.

CONTENTS

	Acknowledgements	vi
	Introduction	vii
1	Journey from Hungary	1
2	Martin Szabados (Mozes Frank)	7
	Ancestors of Martin Szabados	23
	Descendants of Martin & Josephine Szabados	
	son - Erwin Szabados	31
	daughter - Josephine Szabados Clark	123
	son - Fred Szabados	127
	daughter - Marie Szabados Westerdahl	133
	daughter - Suzanne Szabados Myers	139
3	Josephine Szerna	153
	Ancestors of Josephine Szerna	165
4	Birthplaces for Szabados and Szerna Families	211
Appendix A	Elizabeth Takacs Szabados and her ancestors	227
Appendix B	Helen Bedoe Abfalder and her ancestors	289
Appendix C	Leona Oesch and her ancestors	311
Appendix D	Charles Westerdahl and his ancestors	327
Appendix E	Donald Myers and his ancestors	339
Appendix F	DNA Test Results	35/
Appendix G	Hungarian History and Customs	361

Writing Your Family History

For family histories that describe our direct ancestors, I include pedigree or ancestor charts to organize the material and help show the relationships. If the focal point is a grandparent or great-grandparent then charts listing their descendants need to also be used. The charts help everyone keep the relationships clear and the narrative in the family history tells the story.

Here is a standard pedigree chart that I used in one of my family histories. The format that I use for most of my family histories are based on the people listed on this type of chart. Each of the ancestors listed has a summary included in the family history. The summaries for each father is followed by brief summaries for his children and then after the children, I have the summary of the next father. Once I have exhausted the paternal line of ancestors, I begin a summary for each wife of an ancestor and then their fathers. I use slight variations to this format that allows the family story to be told but the pedigree chart supplies the basic outline.

Ancestors of Jedediah Carpenter

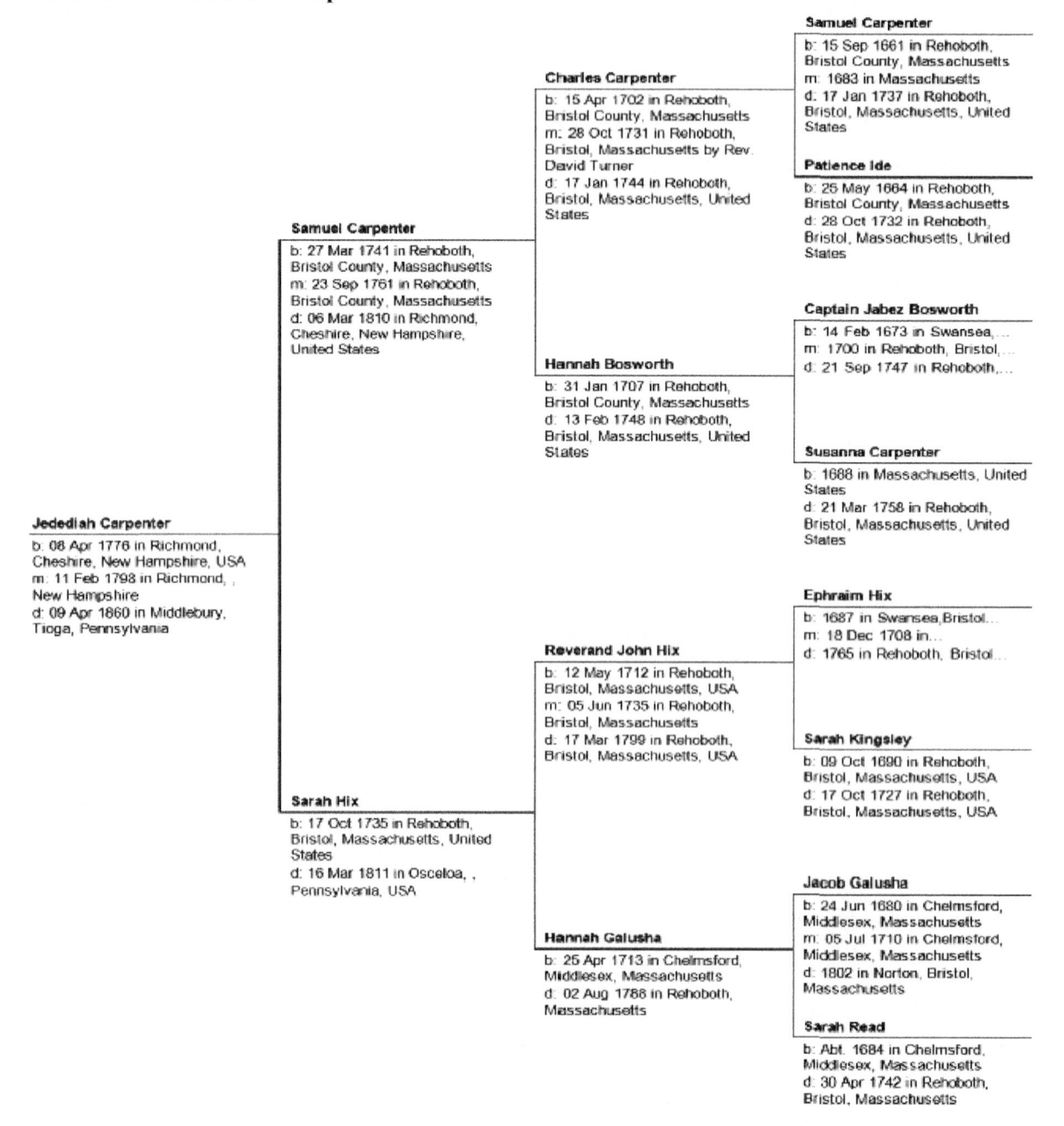

Jedediah Carpenter
b: 08 Apr 1776 in Richmond, Cheshire, New Hampshire, USA
m: 11 Feb 1798 in Richmond, , New Hampshire
d: 09 Apr 1860 in Middlebury, Tioga, Pennsylvania

Samuel Carpenter
b: 27 Mar 1741 in Rehoboth, Bristol County, Massachusetts
m: 23 Sep 1761 in Rehoboth, Bristol County, Massachusetts
d: 06 Mar 1810 in Richmond, Cheshire, New Hampshire, United States

Sarah Hix
b: 17 Oct 1735 in Rehoboth, Bristol, Massachusetts, United States
d: 16 Mar 1811 in Osceloa, , Pennsylvania, USA

Charles Carpenter
b: 15 Apr 1702 in Rehoboth, Bristol County, Massachusetts
m: 28 Oct 1731 in Rehoboth, Bristol, Massachusetts by Rev. David Turner
d: 17 Jan 1744 in Rehoboth, Bristol, Massachusetts, United States

Hannah Bosworth
b: 31 Jan 1707 in Rehoboth, Bristol County, Massachusetts
d: 13 Feb 1748 in Rehoboth, Bristol, Massachusetts, United States

Reverand John Hix
b: 12 May 1712 in Rehoboth, Bristol, Massachusetts, USA
m: 05 Jun 1735 in Rehoboth, Bristol, Massachusetts
d: 17 Mar 1799 in Rehoboth, Bristol, Massachusetts, USA

Hannah Galusha
b: 25 Apr 1713 in Chelmsford, Middlesex, Massachusetts
d: 02 Aug 1788 in Rehoboth, Massachusetts

Samuel Carpenter
b: 15 Sep 1661 in Rehoboth, Bristol County, Massachusetts
m: 1683 in Massachusetts
d: 17 Jan 1737 in Rehoboth, Bristol, Massachusetts, United States

Patience Ide
b: 25 May 1664 in Rehoboth, Bristol County, Massachusetts
d: 28 Oct 1732 in Rehoboth, Bristol, Massachusetts, United States

Captain Jabez Bosworth
b: 14 Feb 1673 in Swansea,...
m: 1700 in Rehoboth, Bristol,...
d: 21 Sep 1747 in Rehoboth,...

Susanna Carpenter
b: 1688 in Massachusetts, United States
d: 21 Mar 1758 in Rehoboth, Bristol, Massachusetts, United States

Ephraim Hix
b: 1687 in Swansea,Bristol...
m: 18 Dec 1708 in...
d: 1765 in Rehoboth, Bristol...

Sarah Kingsley
b: 09 Oct 1690 in Rehoboth, Bristol, Massachusetts, USA
d: 17 Oct 1727 in Rehoboth, Bristol, Massachusetts, USA

Jacob Galusha
b: 24 Jun 1680 in Chelmsford, Middlesex, Massachusetts
m: 05 Jul 1710 in Chelmsford, Middlesex, Massachusetts
d: 1802 in Norton, Bristol, Massachusetts

Sarah Read
b: Abt. 1684 in Chelmsford, Middlesex, Massachusetts
d: 30 Apr 1742 in Rehoboth, Bristol, Massachusetts

More About Writing Family History

Here is a portion of a descendant outline for another of my family histories. Summaries for Silas (#1), his children (#2), his grandchildren (#3) and his great-grandchildren (#4) were included in the family history. By including summaries for the grandchildren and great-grandchildren the size of the family history grew and the audience was also very large.

Outline Descendant Report for Silas Howard

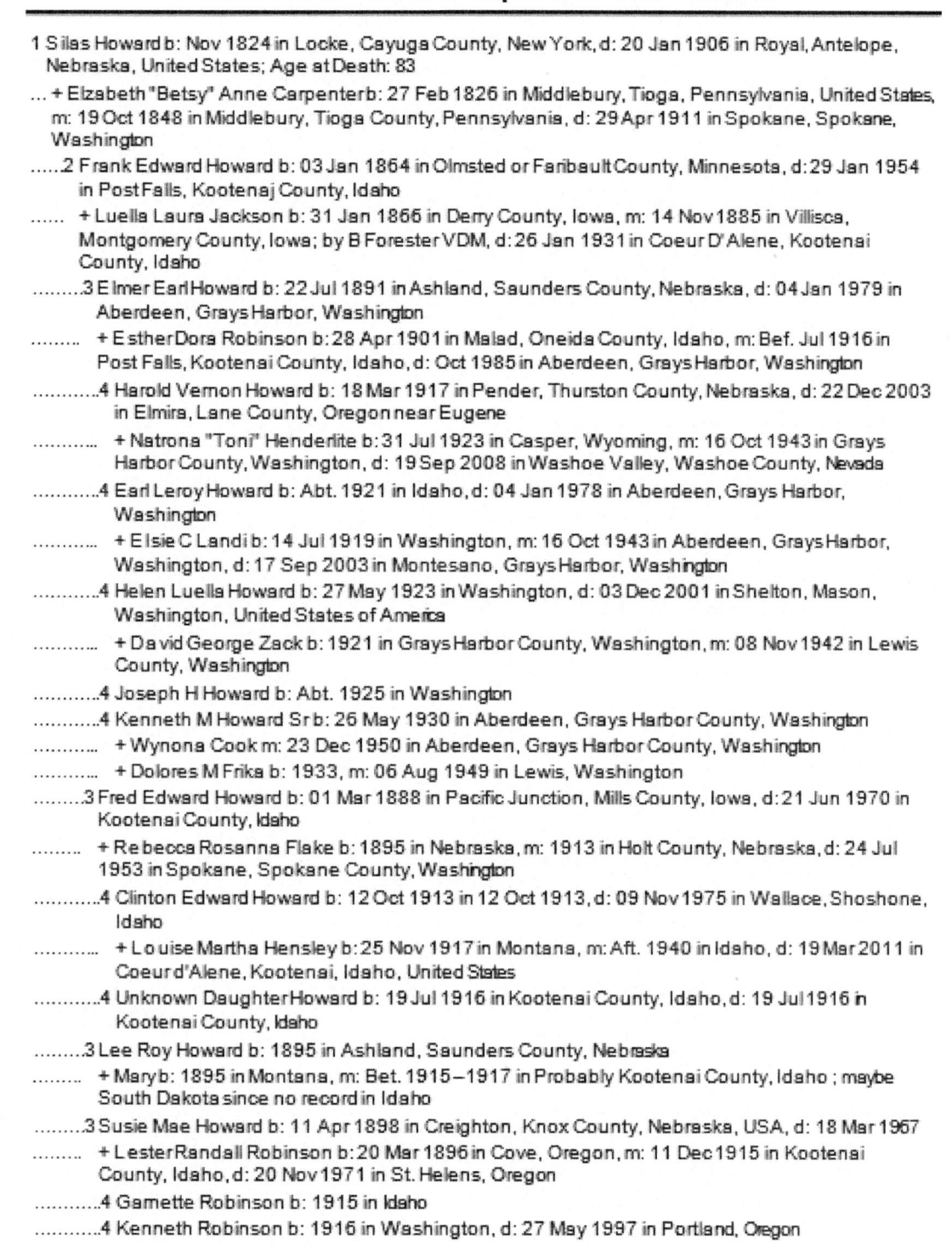

1 Silas Howard b: Nov 1824 in Locke, Cayuga County, New York, d: 20 Jan 1906 in Royal, Antelope, Nebraska, United States; Age at Death: 83
... + Elzabeth "Betsy" Anne Carpenter b: 27 Feb 1826 in Middlebury, Tioga, Pennsylvania, United States, m: 19 Oct 1848 in Middlebury, Tioga County, Pennsylvania, d: 29 Apr 1911 in Spokane, Spokane, Washington
......2 Frank Edward Howard b: 03 Jan 1864 in Olmsted or Faribault County, Minnesota, d: 29 Jan 1954 in Post Falls, Kootenai County, Idaho
...... + Luella Laura Jackson b: 31 Jan 1866 in Derry County, Iowa, m: 14 Nov 1885 in Villisca, Montgomery County, Iowa; by B Forester VDM, d: 26 Jan 1931 in Coeur D'Alene, Kootenai County, Idaho
.........3 Elmer Earl Howard b: 22 Jul 1891 in Ashland, Saunders County, Nebraska, d: 04 Jan 1979 in Aberdeen, Grays Harbor, Washington
.... + Esther Dora Robinson b: 28 Apr 1901 in Malad, Oneida County, Idaho, m: Bef. Jul 1916 in Post Falls, Kootenai County, Idaho, d: Oct 1985 in Aberdeen, Grays Harbor, Washington
............4 Harold Vernon Howard b: 18 Mar 1917 in Pender, Thurston County, Nebraska, d: 22 Dec 2003 in Elmira, Lane County, Oregon near Eugene
.... + Natrona "Toni" Henderlite b: 31 Jul 1923 in Casper, Wyoming, m: 16 Oct 1943 in Grays Harbor County, Washington, d: 19 Sep 2008 in Washoe Valley, Washoe County, Nevada
............4 Earl Leroy Howard b: Abt. 1921 in Idaho, d: 04 Jan 1978 in Aberdeen, Grays Harbor, Washington
.... + Elsie C Landi b: 14 Jul 1919 in Washington, m: 16 Oct 1943 in Aberdeen, Grays Harbor, Washington, d: 17 Sep 2003 in Montesano, Grays Harbor, Washington
............4 Helen Luella Howard b: 27 May 1923 in Washington, d: 03 Dec 2001 in Shelton, Mason, Washington, United States of America
.... + David George Zack b: 1921 in Grays Harbor County, Washington, m: 08 Nov 1942 in Lewis County, Washington
............4 Joseph H Howard b: Abt. 1925 in Washington
............4 Kenneth M Howard Sr b: 26 May 1930 in Aberdeen, Grays Harbor County, Washington
.... + Wynona Cook m: 23 Dec 1950 in Aberdeen, Grays Harbor County, Washington
.... + Dolores M Frika b: 1933, m: 06 Aug 1949 in Lewis, Washington
.........3 Fred Edward Howard b: 01 Mar 1888 in Pacific Junction, Mills County, Iowa, d: 21 Jun 1970 in Kootenai County, Idaho
.... + Rebecca Rosanna Flake b: 1895 in Nebraska, m: 1913 in Holt County, Nebraska, d: 24 Jul 1953 in Spokane, Spokane County, Washington
............4 Clinton Edward Howard b: 12 Oct 1913 in 12 Oct 1913, d: 09 Nov 1975 in Wallace, Shoshone, Idaho
.... + Louise Martha Hensley b: 25 Nov 1917 in Montana, m: Aft. 1940 in Idaho, d: 19 Mar 2011 in Coeur d'Alene, Kootenai, Idaho, United States
............4 Unknown Daughter Howard b: 19 Jul 1916 in Kootenai County, Idaho, d: 19 Jul 1916 in Kootenai County, Idaho
.........3 Lee Roy Howard b: 1895 in Ashland, Saunders County, Nebraska
.... + Mary b: 1895 in Montana, m: Bet. 1915–1917 in Probably Kootenai County, Idaho ; maybe South Dakota since no record in Idaho
.........3 Susie Mae Howard b: 11 Apr 1898 in Creighton, Knox County, Nebraska, USA, d: 18 Mar 1967
.... + Lester Randall Robinson b: 20 Mar 1896 in Cove, Oregon, m: 11 Dec 1915 in Kootenai County, Idaho, d: 20 Nov 1971 in St. Helens, Oregon
............4 Garnette Robinson b: 1915 in Idaho
............4 Kenneth Robinson b: 1916 in Washington, d: 27 May 1997 in Portland, Oregon

Are you writing about the descendants of one ancestor?
Some family histories have been written that have made a distant ancestors from the 1400 or 1500s as the focal point. The histories then trace their descendants down through many generations. This is a very complicated format to write and also to read. The history starts with the founding ancestors as number 1. Their children are listed and also assigned a succeeding number if they are mentioned in the next generation. Generally the oldest child will have the smallest number. However, if the grandchildren are assigned numbers, their number is based when their parent is discussed. Therefore the oldest son of son #2 may have a larger number than the youngest son of son #1 because the next generation is numbered sequentially by the order their parent is listed. Each generation of children is listed in the section for their generation and included by the number that was assigned to them. I find this system very complicated to follow as I read these histories.

Although, I find this format difficult to read, I have found the information covered in some very useful to include in the family histories that I write. Some are only a list of relationships and others contain interesting information for some of the people listed. However, I am careful to depend on only the histories that have been reliably sourced to make sure the information is accurate. Two reliable and well accepted books helped me document my son-in-law's connection to Mayflower passengers.

Historical references can also be used to identify famous distant relatives that share a distant common ancestor. In my son-in-law's family tree he has Mayflower passengers John and Elizabeth Howland as direct ancestors. Notable descendants of these two ancestors include U.S. presidents Franklin D. Roosevelt, George H. W. Bush, and George W. Bush; U.S. first ladies Edith Roosevelt and Barbara Bush; poets Ralph Waldo Emerson, Henry Wadsworth Longfellow, Mormon prophet and founder of the Church of Jesus Christ of Latter-day Saints Joseph Smith, Jr. and his wife Emma Hale; Mormon leader Brigham Young; Continental Congress president Nathaniel Gorham; former Alaska Governor Sarah Palin; former Florida governor Jeb Bush; and actors/actresses Humphrey Bogart, Maude Adams, Lillian Russell and Anthony Perkins. Although this list is very interesting to mention in the section for John Howland, I feel it is only an interesting item for casual conversation.

Write about one ancestor
The last format that I want to discuss is writing about only one ancestor. If you are interested in Revolutionary War history, you may find writing about one ancestor who fought in the Revolutionary War will expand your knowledge of the history of the war and also provide an interesting story for the family. Other possible candidates for a single person history would be the military of other wars, early settlers of areas, ancestors who traveled the Oregon Trail, others who may have gone to California for the Gold Rush of 1850 or someone that was a hero. If your family has one story that has persisted over many generations, investigating the circumstances would be a candidate for this type of story.

My son-in-law had an ancestor that left Michigan to join the California Gold Rush but then ran pack trains to the miners in Washington. He then retired to manage orchards in Oregon. He was an early settle in Union County Oregon and I found a short sketch of his life in the history for Union County. Since he was alive at the time the history was written, I surmise that he may have been interviewed for his sketch. From the information that I have found for him, he would be a very good candidate for a one person history.

The Index

An index is a detailed alphabetical listing of the names, places, topics and the page numbers for each item. They are designed to help the reader find information quickly and easily. The index should not only include names and places but should also include a list of subjects. For a family history, an index is not optional. The list of names will help family members quickly lookup the pages that cover specific ancestors and help find the favorite stories to read.

Indexes can be created manually or automatically. When it is created manually, the list of names, places and topics is created and then the text is reviewed to add the correct page number where the material appears. Some word processing programs such as Microsoft Word allow for embedding codes that tag the words and locations to be included in index list. After the location and words are tagged, the index can be created automatically. The page numbers can automatically be updated if the content is revised and page numbers change. Using embedded indexing tags may save time in the long-run when the document is revised and repagination is needed.

Copyrights

Understanding copyright laws is important not only to protect what you have written but also to ensure that you have not infringed upon the rights of others. A copyright is a legal device that provides the creator of a work of art or literature the right to control how it is used. For our purposes the copyright includes the right to make and distribute copies of the work.

Once you write your family history, you become the copyright holder as soon as you put into a fixed form such as a published book. Other examples would be a type manuscript, an eBook and a CD. Your work does not have to been registered with the Copyright Office. Your work is protected from the moment you put your work in fixed form. If you are distributing your family history only to your family members, you may not want to register your work. However, if you want to investigate more about registration, the instructions and forms to register your work can be obtained online at www.loc.gov/copyright. The fee is about $30 and will require submitting two copies of your book with the forms.

The same rights that protect you also protect authors that may have produced information that you use in your family history.

Copyrights do not last forever. If the work was produce on or after January 1, 1978, the copyright protection is for the life of the author plus seventy years. If the work was create before 1923, it is now in the public domain and can be used without the author's permission. For works created between 1923 and 1978, different rules apply. The 1978 revision to the copyright law changed the duration for works produced between 1923 and 1978 for a maximum of 56 years to 75 years or 90 years depending on how the work was produced.

When in doubt its best to ask for permission to reprint something.
- For a work published commercially, write the publisher for permission
- For a work that was self published, ask the author.
- For periodicals, ask the editor.
- For photographs, track down the photographer.
- For items found in a newspaper, contact the editor of the newspaper.

The Experience of Writing My Family Histories
After I had written my family histories, I realized that I had gone through a number of phases in my thought process to get it written. My initial goals were to find out more about my Polish and Hungarian family history. As I was finalizing the word file for publishing and distributing to my cousins, my goal had expanded to include saving the information that I found by producing multiple printed copies for my family. When I started my research, I could not envision myself as a writer and I could not believe that I had the organizational and writing skills to do such an important writing project. Somehow my research methods produced biographical narratives in small sections that could be combined to produce family histories that are being enjoyed by many family members.

The key was focusing on doing the research and writing summaries to share with family members. These small pieces could eventually be combined into a great family history.

The various stages in developing my family history were:
1. Research and start compiling summaries

    I began using summaries to make my research efforts be more efficient. My summaries listed the facts that I had found for a person and reduced the time needed to enter information into new online search pages. The summary would also be a quick reference to show what information I had and were missing for each individual. I believe that my summaries proved to be the most important tool for my research process.

    Initially the summaries were a personal tool for me. Bullet points were used to enter information and grammar and complete sentences were not important.

    I would recommend that you begin writing now. Do not hesitate because of any anxieties you might have about writing. It's time to get the information, stories, feelings, and outcomes recorded. Initially, do not worry about style, grammar, and punctuation. You can polish your writing later.

    As you review your work and find something that does not seem to fit, do not be afraid to delete this section. However, save this deleted information in spare parts file in case you decide to reinstate it later.

2. Show summaries and pictures to family members

    After I started compiling my summaries I found the added benefit that they were a great tool when sharing my research with my family. Since they were more readable than the documents, more relatives were interested in reviewing my research and this generated more family members contributing stories, documents and pictures.

3. Insert copies of pictures and documents into summaries

    Initially I included copies of pictures and documents as pages behind the summaries in my ring binder. When I started emailing my research to distant cousins, I found it was more convenient to combine the summaries, pictures and documents into one document and send them a PDF file. The PDFs could be for one individual or be for a group of individuals. Once the enlarged summaries were created, I updated the new documents and not the original summaries. If I combined a group of individuals, text was added to organize the group and to transition between the different sections. Summaries that included pictures and documents were a small step towards the family history pages. The group documents were a larger step towards the creation of my family history.

This step was to exchange information with distant relatives but indirectly helped in the creation of my family history.

4. Begin using only one word document as my summary
   Eventually the various summaries that I was updating emerged as one family history document. The stories that emerged in each summary became related and needed to be merged and organized together. Additional sections for immigration and birthplaces were easy to add at this stage of the work. Most of the research work was done but more would be added as this was shared with the family and more information was contributed. Reading the history would also generate more questions that required more research that would tell a more complete story.

   Small stories that emerged from the individual summaries cascaded into the wonderful family history that the family can now enjoy.

5. Decide to publish and share information with family members
   When I felt I had found most of the available information for my family history, I decided to publish it in a bound book because I felt this format may be saved by more people over time. I wanted the pictures, documents and stories that I found to survive.

   Another reason that I recommend to consider for the publication of material would be to celebrate an event such as a family reunion or anniversary.

6. The next step was to decide who the audience was and then organize the format.
   The family members who would be reading my family histories affected the format and order of when and in what section individuals would appear in the family history.

   My family on my mother's side consisted of only my sister and myself. Therefore, my mother's family had a simple order starting with my mother, then listing her father and his ancestors. Next I listed her mother Anna and then Anna's ancestors. In comparison, my dad's family consisted of many first and second cousins and most of them contributed information to the history. I started this history with my great-grandparents because they were the common ancestors for all of the surviving cousins. I then listed the descendants who included their children and grandchildren. After the sections for their descendants, I started tracing the ancestors for my great-grandfather and then my great-grandmother.

   The second format is more complicated but has a focus that appeals to all of the cousins.

CHAPTER SIX – BEYOND THE BASICS:
Pictures, Illustrations, Maps, Timelines and Social History

As I stated earlier, our genealogy research should be more than collecting documents. The documents tell a story and your genealogy research can generate a family history that will be a wonderful treasure for many future generations of your family.

As I started compiling the information from the documents, I found that pictures added an interest and a great visual explanation to the stories. Seeing pictures of my ancestors and the homes made my family history come alive. I added maps and timelines which also helped tell the family story. I also had questions about their immigration and their birthplaces which I tried to answer with sections describing these two elements in their lives. I added a section on the customs and traditions of my Hungarian and Polish ancestors in an attempt to help explain these parts of our heritage to my grandchildren. Adding these elements seems to bring out their human aspects and reveal more of their lives.

In this chapter, I review tips that I used to incorporate these elements in my family histories. I use Microsoft Word to write my family histories but most word processing software should have the functions that I will discuss in the following pages.

Pictures

Photos are a very important for your family history because they provide a visual record of your ancestors and may provide information for your family history that was not recorded in any documents.. When photos are added to the text they bring the stories alive. Adding pictures of your ancestors and other family members makes the words more personal. Your photos may document many events in their lives such as the birth of a child, weddings, school graduations, and holidays are just a few of the possible photo opportunities. If these pictures are not in the albums of your close family members seeking more distant relatives. Wills rarely list who inherits the family photographs and saving them depend on the mercy and interest of the relatives. Seek out the people who were the caregivers when your ancestors died. This was usually the oldest daughter but it also could have been a daughter who did not marry or a child that lived near-by. Go beyond the pictures of people and also use photos that show their homes, neighborhoods, occupations and cemetery markers. Here you may have to travel to take pictures of the "old homestead", places of employment and cemeteries. If the building has been torn down, look in the picture files at the local libraries or historical museums. You may also find these background pictures found on internet at websites for the county, county historical societies or county genealogical societies. Printed material such as magazines and books may also yield pictures of your ancestors. Do not overlook professional journals that may have recorded any awards or recognition that they may have received. Newspapers may also contain pictures of your ancestors if they participated in a local or national event or they were included in a story of local interest. You may also find pictures that relate to your ancestors on the websites for Find a grave, Ancient Faces, Dead Fred or through contacts that you may find on message board at Genforum.com and on Rootsweb.com.

Writing Your Family History

One of my goals after my mother died was to scan the pictures in her scrapbook and share copies with my sister. I also wanted to identify who was in the pictures and label them to pass this along to my children. An added benefit of scanning the pictures was making them available to be included in my family histories which now became scrapbooks also. Inserting pictures next to specific narrative will add an image to the words and add interest to the family history. I try to include pictures of all of the homes where the family lived, churches where they were baptized and married, places where they worked and pictures of their grave markers. Any pictures related to specific events such as wedding pictures were inserted next to the pertinent narrative.

Besides using my mother's scrapbook, I obtained family pictures from my cousins that added further to the family. Initially, I traveled to take pictures of residences and cemetery grave markers. Now, I use the street view function of Google maps to obtain pictures of homes. I also search Wikipedia, county websites and historical/genealogy society websites for pictures that may add interest to the stories in your family history. I used ancestry.com for pictures of the ships that my ancestors used to immigrate to America.

Here is a list of pictures and illustrations that I try to include in my family histories.
- Vintage pictures from family albums showing as many relatives and ancestors as possible.
- Pictures of homes
- Pictures or illustrations of the ships the immigrants were on when they arrived
- Pictures of churches
- Pictures of grade schools, high schools and colleges where your family members attended
- Picture of any artifact that is connected to your ancestors
- Pictures of cemeteries graves markers
- Vintage pictures of "old county" villages
- Maps showing the location of birthplaces
- Maps showing migration routes
- Copies of all documents – birth, marriage, death, census, passenger, naturalization, land, probate, obituaries
- Pictures, maps and illustrations about any military service or action connected to our ancestors.
- Pictures of place of employment and pictures depicting type of work.
- Stock pictures depicting any important activities in their life.

If you find a picture or illustration that depicts some aspect of your ancestor's life that is not included in the above list please use it.

Identifying when a picture was taken will help identify what you need to know from the photo. If there is someone that you know in the picture what is their approximate age? The age of children are easier to estimate with a narrower range. How are they dressed and can their clothes date the picture? Is the picture taken at the time of a major event – baptism, graduation, wedding or death that mark when it was taken? What is the type of picture – daguerreotype, tintypes, cabinet card, etc? Each type was used during specific periods. If the photo was done by a professional, when was he in business?

What buildings, landscape or street marking are shown in a picture. These items will help identify where the picture was taken. If a building that is shown was later torn down will also help date the picture. Look for other items in the picture that may identify the event. Wedding dresses are obvious but many brides could not avoid such a specialized dress but may be in their best dress and holding a bouquet in their wedding portraits. Children dressed in white suits or dresses for their first communion. Groups of children surrounding a table and supervised by adults may be a birthday party. If there is a car in the picture, look at the license plates to see if the year can been seen.

In group photos, compare the people you do know to those that you do not know. How are they dressed? Can you estimate their approximate ages? Where was it taken and when was family there? Are there heirloom items such as paintings in the background?

Some pictures have people, places and events that cannot be identified. Successfully identifying these pictures can yield more family information for the family history.

Who are these people? In the picture on the right is my mother, grandmother and sister with two unknown women. My mother is pregnant with me so the picture was taken in the spring of 1947. Using the street sign and the line of building in the background on the left, the corner has been identified as East Ohio Street and North Ada Street in Chicago. The photographer is looking eastward.

Who are the two unknown women. They may be distant relatives of my grandmother or grandfather who may have just immigrated from Poland. I still have no clues to their names and further research is needed to identify them.

In my search for these pictures, I have been reunited with family members that I have not seen since childhood.

My mother, grandmother, my sister (front) and two unknown women at Ada and Ohio streets in Chicago

Writing Your Family History

Below is a sample of two pages from my family history showing how I incorporated pictures into the narrative. Note that the pictures are labeled, inserted next to or after the appropriate text. On the next three pages are examples incorporating pictures with documents.

The first example shows a picture of my grandfather in his WW I Army uniform. I found this picture in my mother's photo album. Also note that the picture shows a plaque at his foot that indicates his regiment and company. The second picture shows Camp Wadsworth and I found this picture in an article on Wikipedia on the camp.

Citizenship and WW I

The United States declared war against Germany and the Axis countries on April 6, 1917 and Steve enlisted in the US Army on May 11, 1917 in Chicago. Steve listed his sister Mary Lapinska as his closest relative (Mary's address was listed at 1324 Holt Street in Chicago). His enlistment papers were signed by Major C.E. Freeman. His service number was #745524. His grave marker indicated that he was a member of the Illinois Mechanized Division.

He was initially sent to Jefferson Barracks in Missouri for classification and assignment. On May 18, 1917, he was assigned to the 6th Infantry Division, Company K, 54th regiment at El Paso, Texas (Fort Bliss). Note the small sign by his left foot in the picture to the left (K 54 for Company K, 54th regiment). His service records indicated that he attained the rifleman's classification. Sometime in 1918, his unit was transferred to Camp Wadsworth in Spartenburg, South Carolina. This was probably in preparation for deployment to Europe.

Steve Zuchowski in training

His wife's naturalization papers listed that Steve was naturalized on June 22, 1918 in Spartenburg, South Carolina *on Certificate 1015339*. Spartenburg was the location of Camp Wadsworth from 1917 to 1919.

His pay records indicated that he received 421 days of pay before he arrived in Europe. This would indicate that he arrived in Europe in July 1918.

Camp Wadsworth, South Carolina

70

Beyond the Basics

The next example shows information about my grandmother's death. There is a picture of her marker that I took. I also included a map of the cemetery and a scanned copy of her death certificate.

St Mary's Cemetery, Bloomington, Illinois – section A

Death Certificate for Anna Zuchowski, Died January 4, 1965

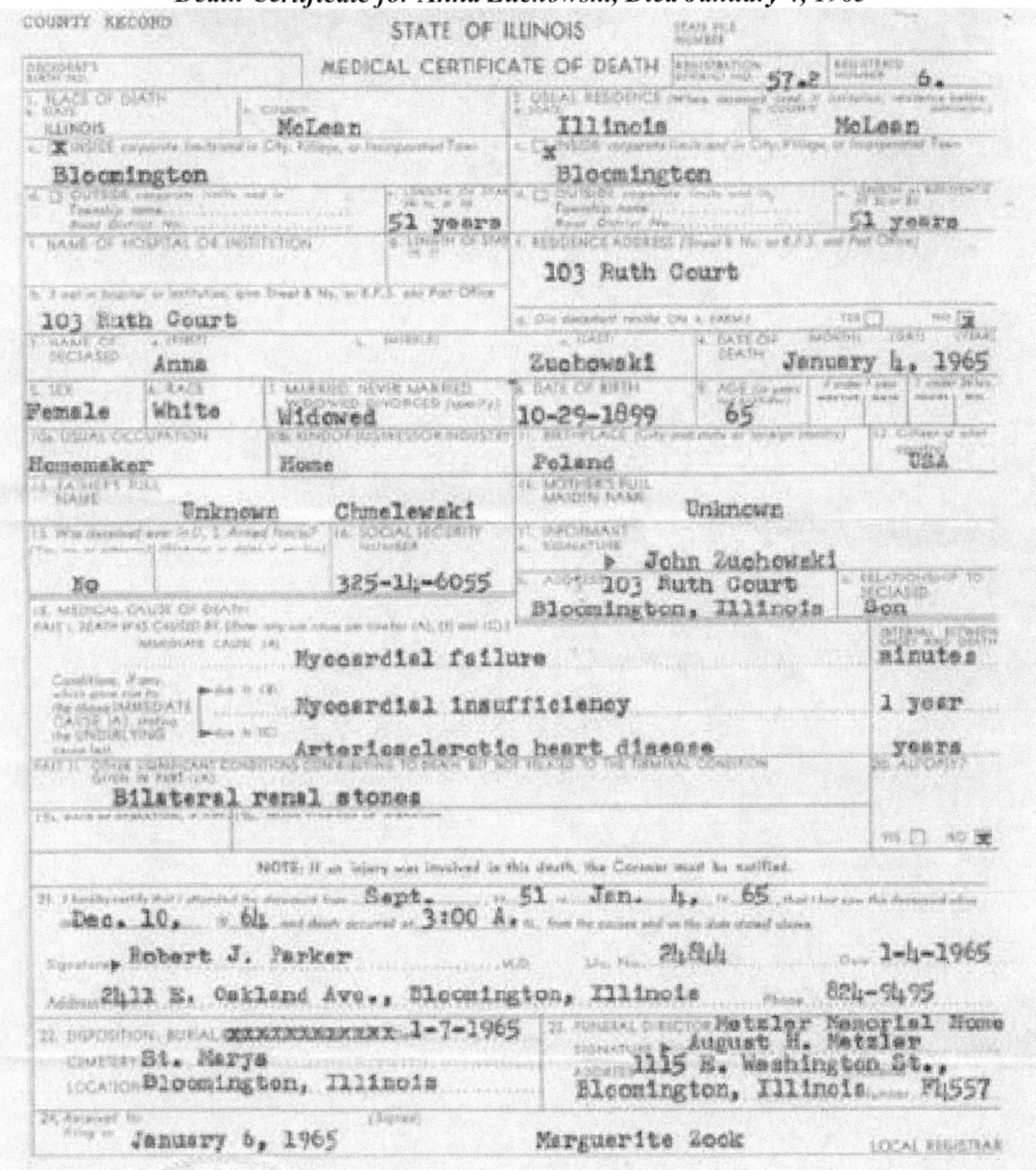

71

This next example shows a copy of my grandfather's baptismal certificate and a picture of the church in Poland where he was baptized. I found the certificate in my mother's files and found the picture of the church on the internet

Baptismal Certificate for Steve John Zuchowski
December 26, 1893

St Peter and Paul the Apostles Church, Czyzew, Poland

Beyond the Basics

The last example shows the two pages of my Grandfather's passenger manifest and a picture of the ship that carried him to Philadelphia. I found both on Ancestry.com

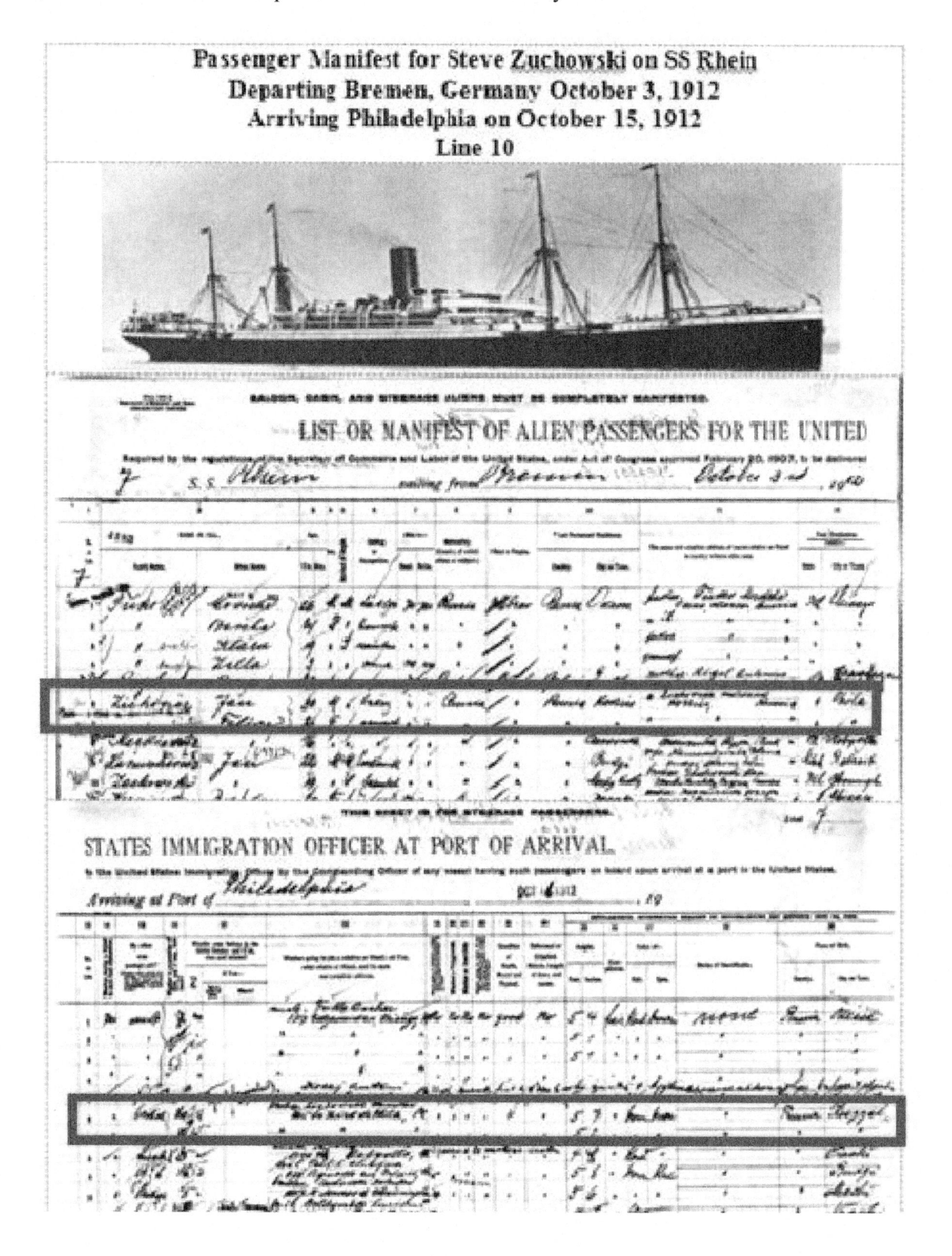

Inserting Pictures

The key to inserting pictures into your family history is the use of the tables. A table is a grid of *cells* arranged in *rows* (horizontal) and *columns (vertical)* to organize data. The grid of rows and columns allows portions of the page to be sectioned off and control the positioning of information. A table allows formatting a page with text next to a picture. The current versions of most word processing programs allows placing text next to pictures without using tables but I recommend using tables because a table will allow me to be more precise in positioning the combination of text and pictures. I view each cell as a separate page and this is why I feel I have better control of the appearance of the entire page.

In the sample page shown below note that I have inserted a table that has two rows and two columns. One cell has text and the other three cells have family pictures with text labels. Having separate cells allows me to left justify the text of the narrative and then center the text for the labels under the pictures. The labeling of pictures becomes difficult if a table is not used.

Portion of family history page
Note grid lines indicating table with two rows and two columns

In March 1955, Martin and Regina purchased the lot west of 1409 W Mulberry from her parents for $100 and built a new house. Marty installed all the electrical and plumbing work for the new house and he traded labor with the painter at the hospital who painted the interior of the house and stained the woodwork. This lot had been included with the purchase of the house at 1409 W Mulberry and the city assigned the address as 1409 ½ because it was located between 1409 and 1411 W Mulberry. The two lots may have been for the addresses of 1407 & 1409 W Mulberry but the first house was numbered incorrectly in 1831 as 1409 W Mulberry.

1409 ½ W Mulberry on the left and 1409 W Mulberry on the right

Marty with son Steve in drive of 1409 W Mulberry

Marty and Steve at Long Lake Wisconsin – about 1960

Beyond the Basics

Steps to insert a table in Microsoft Word
1. Use insert tab on Word tool bar and select table.
2. A command box will pop-up to select the number of rows and columns.. I normally use two columns and one to three rows.
3. After clicking "OK" in the command box, the grid will appear on the page. You can begin inserting information in each cell.
4. Note that the grid will show a black border. After you have entered the information and pictures, you can make the black border disappear by using the table tools at the top of the Word tool bars and selecting "no borders"

See Illustrations below:

Step 1 - Insert Table

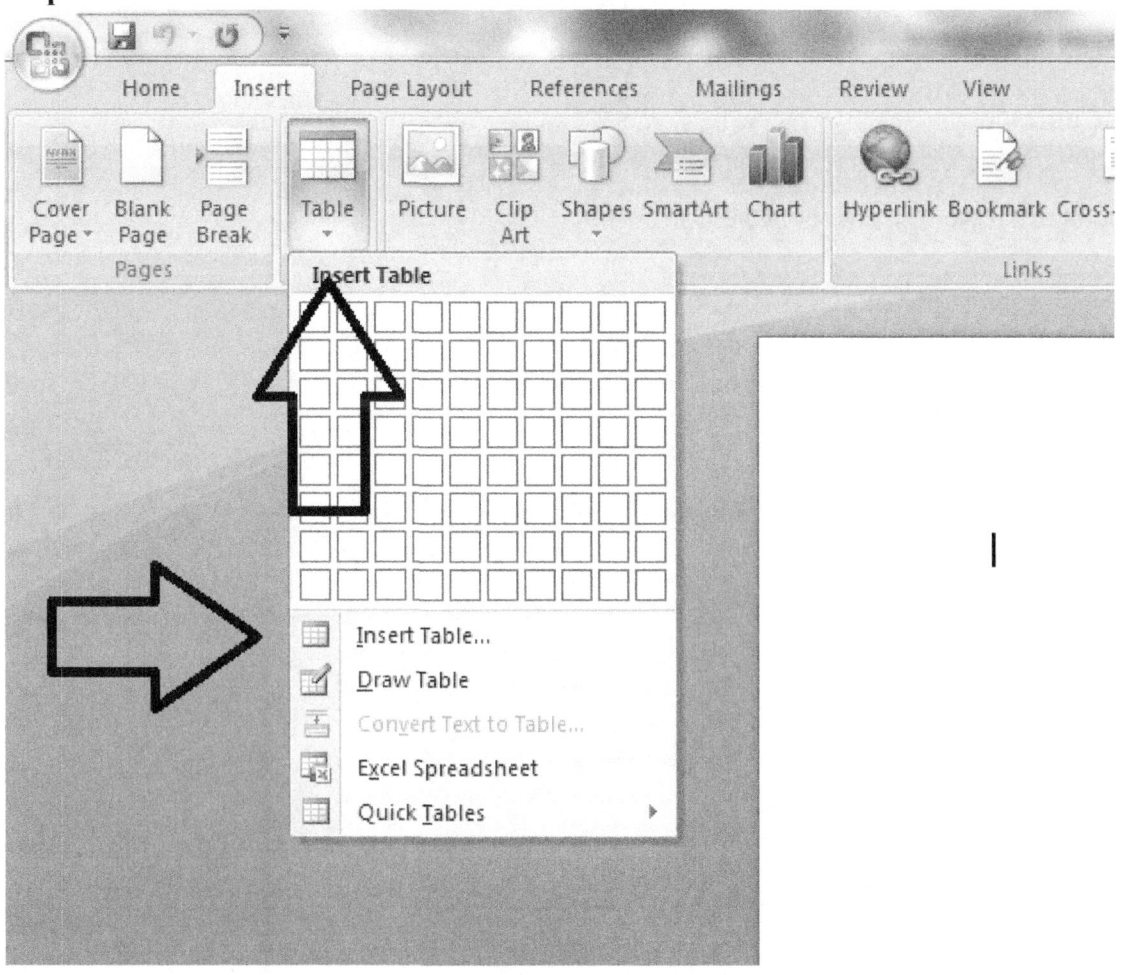

Step 2 - Select number of rows and columns

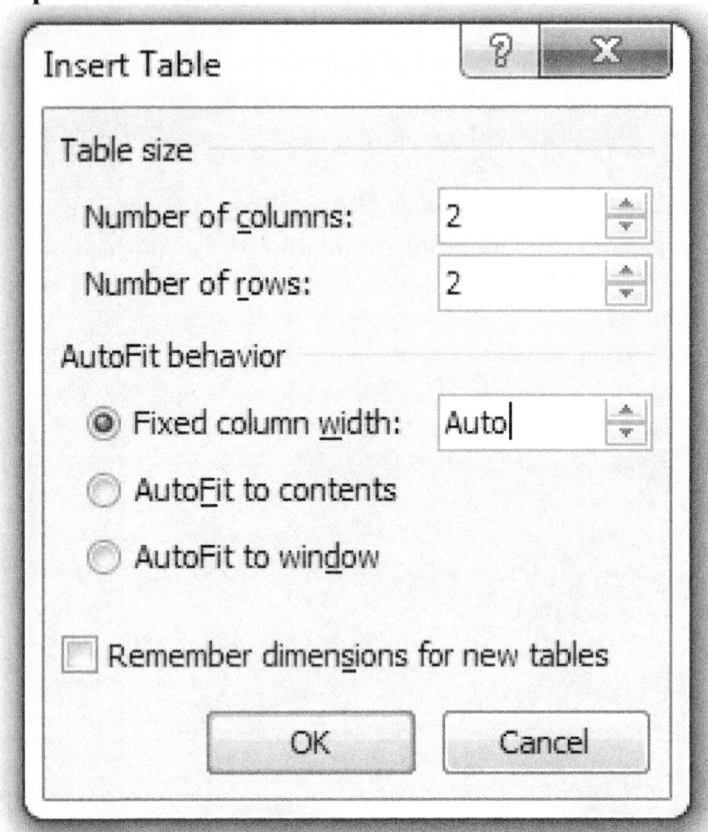

Step 3 - Insert information into cells

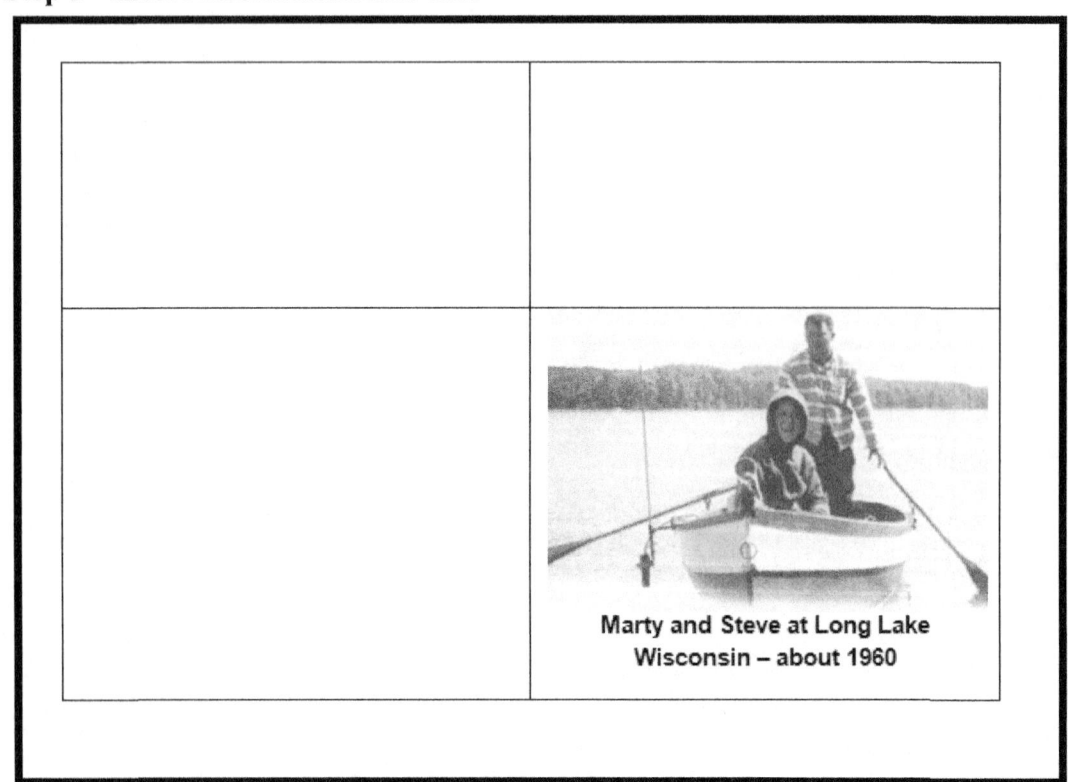

Marty and Steve at Long Lake Wisconsin – about 1960

Beyond the Basics

Use Maps to show locations and explain migration.

I use maps to help explain many aspects of the family history. General maps will help show the locations of birthplaces. Migration maps will show birthplaces, routes to the port of departure and port of arrival. A migration map can also how the timeline and locations as a family branch moves across the United States. I have also found that a city map marking the various addresses where the family lived adds a very interesting visual picture for the reader. The next few pages will show you examples of these various maps and then I will explain how to add text, arrows and lines to existing maps.

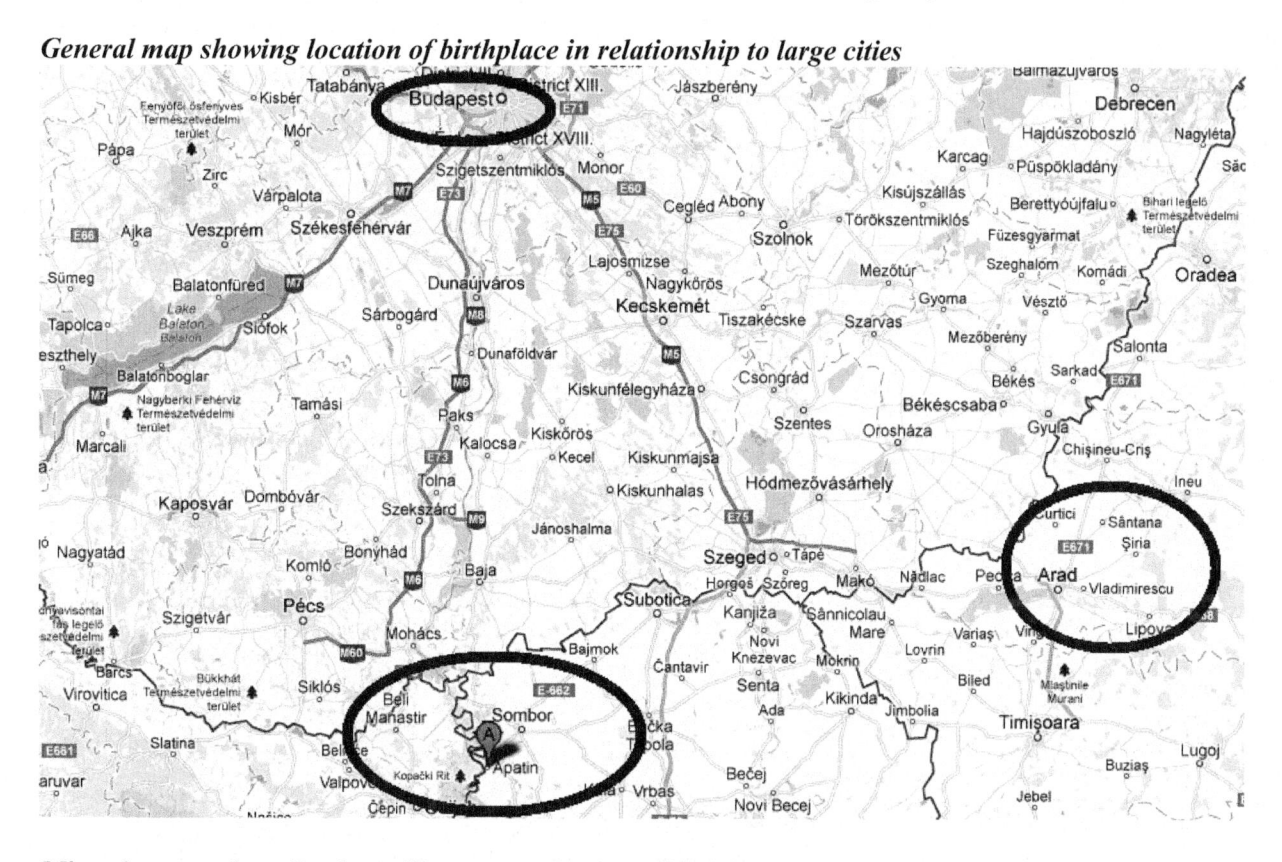

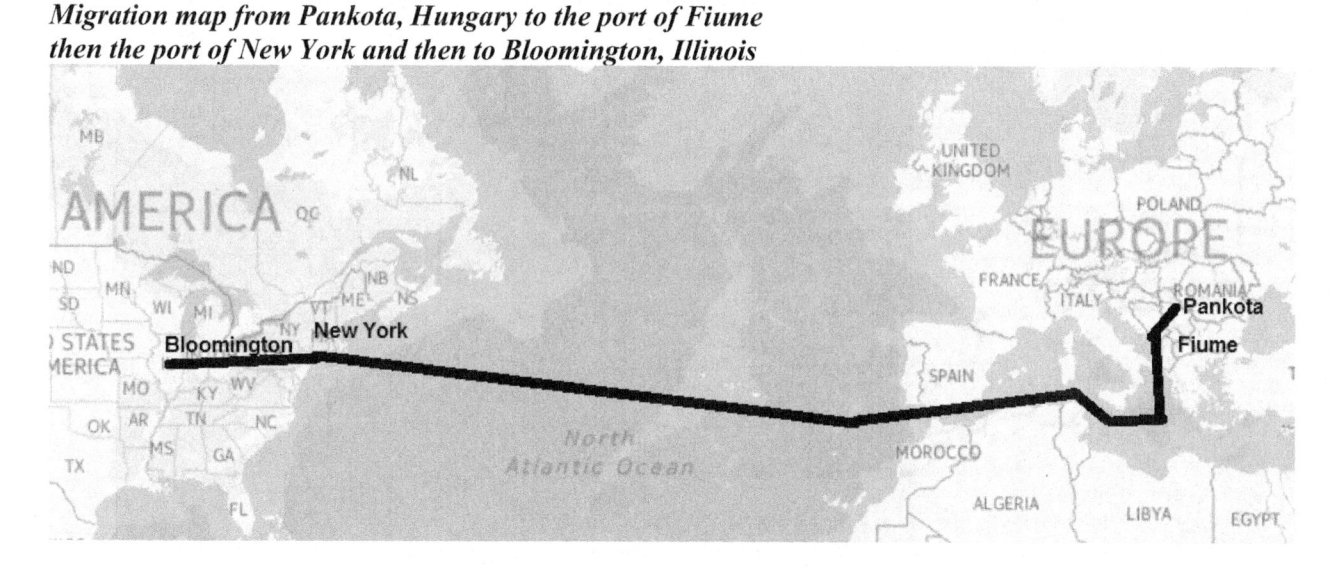

General map showing location of birthplace in relationship to large cities

*Migration map from Pankota, Hungary to the port of Fiume
then the port of New York and then to Bloomington, Illinois*

Migration map for family across the U.S. in the 1700s and 1800s
(this can also be called a timeline)

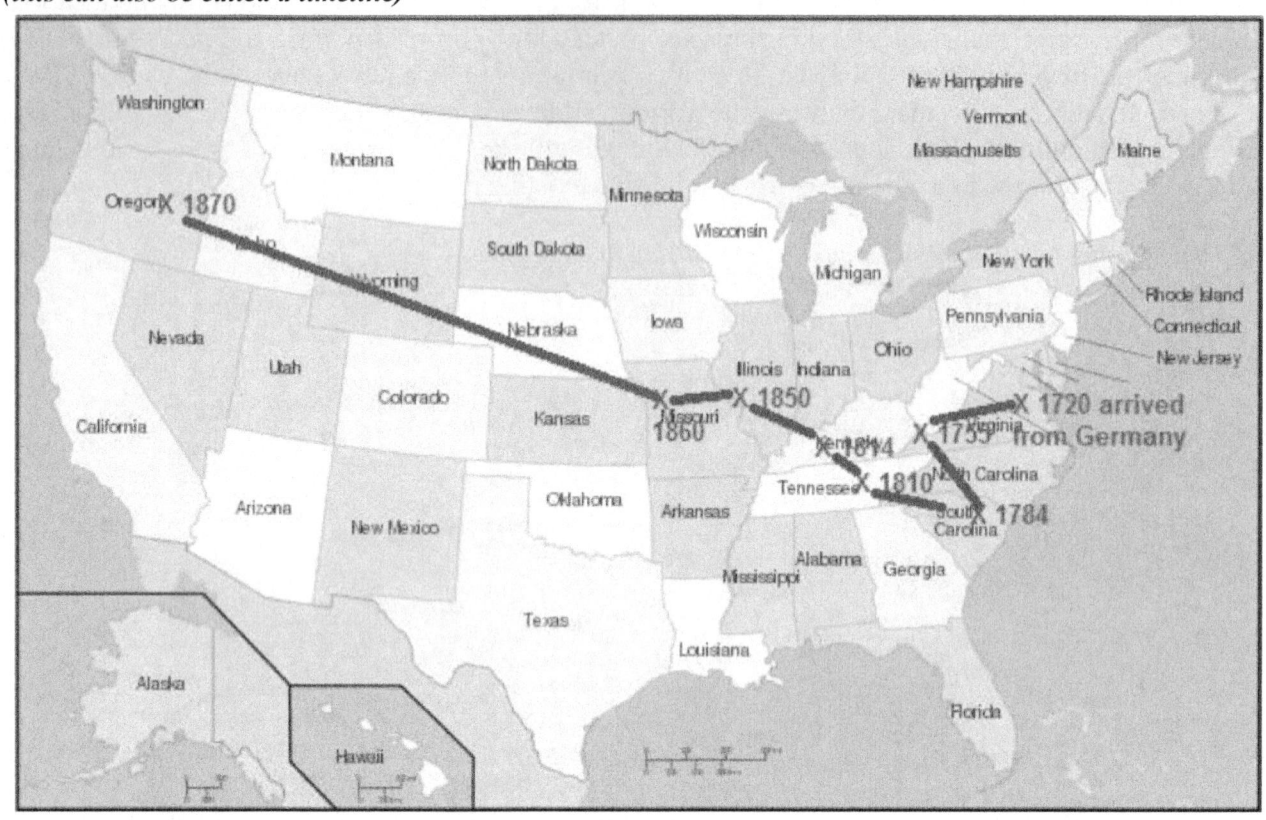

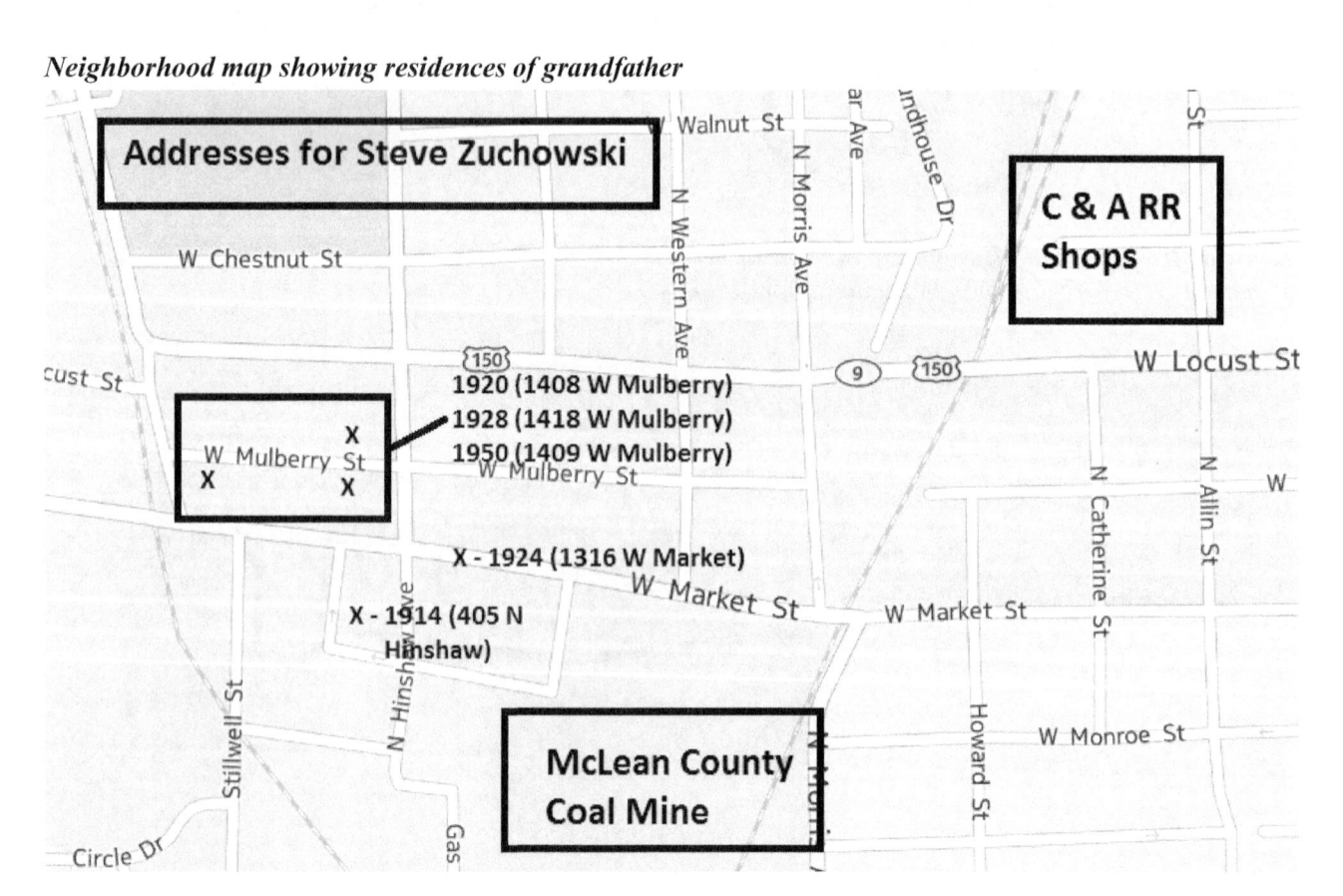

Neighborhood map showing residences of grandfather

Beyond the Basics

How to customize existing maps

1. Find existing map that will show pertinent areas – Wikipedia.com, Scan of personal map or screen print of online map.
2. Copy and paste map into picture editing program. I use Microsoft Paint that was included with my computer software.
3. Use the text function to locate and label points of interest on map.
4. Select the "line" icon in the shapes tool box and draw lines between each point.
5. Other shapes that I use is the "box", "oval" and "arrows" to highlight various areas on the map

See Illustrations below:

Step 3 - Use the text function to locate and label points

Step 4 - Draw lines between each point

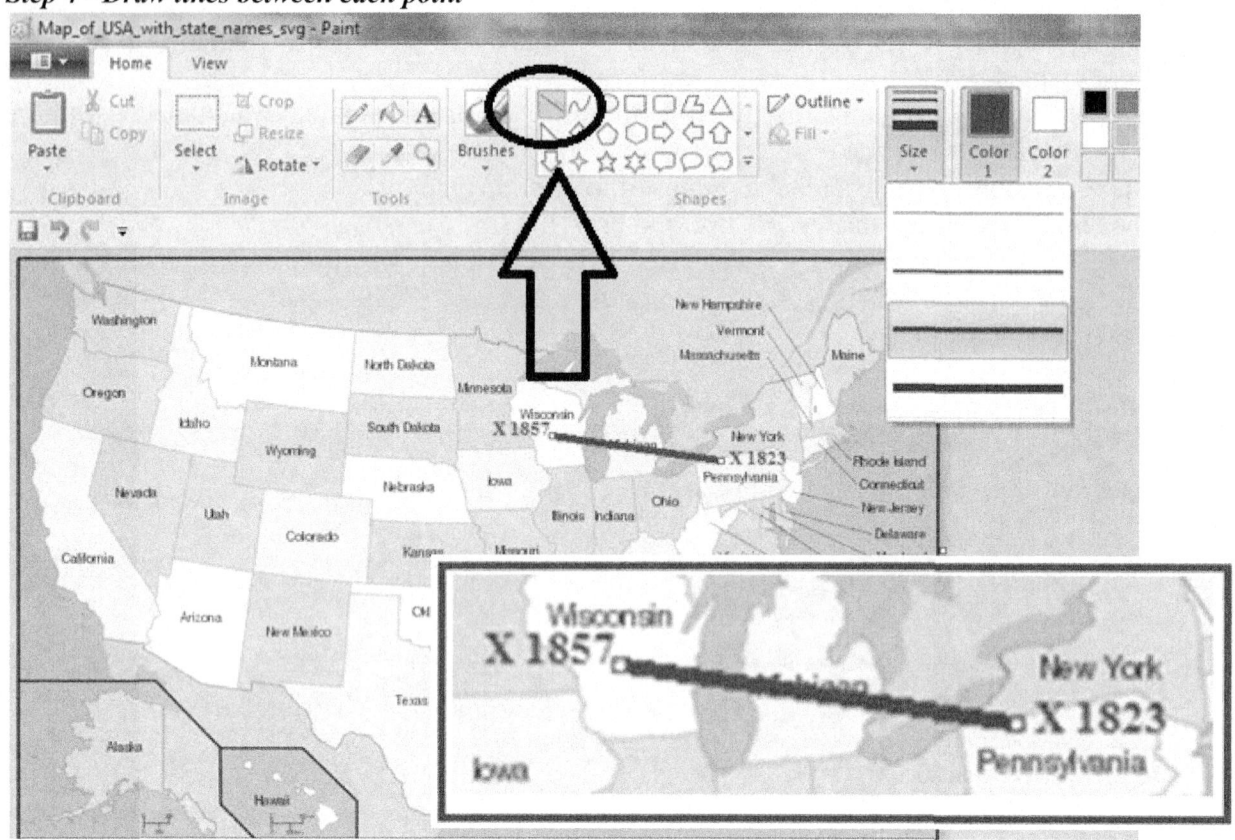

Step 5 - Tool Bar Icons

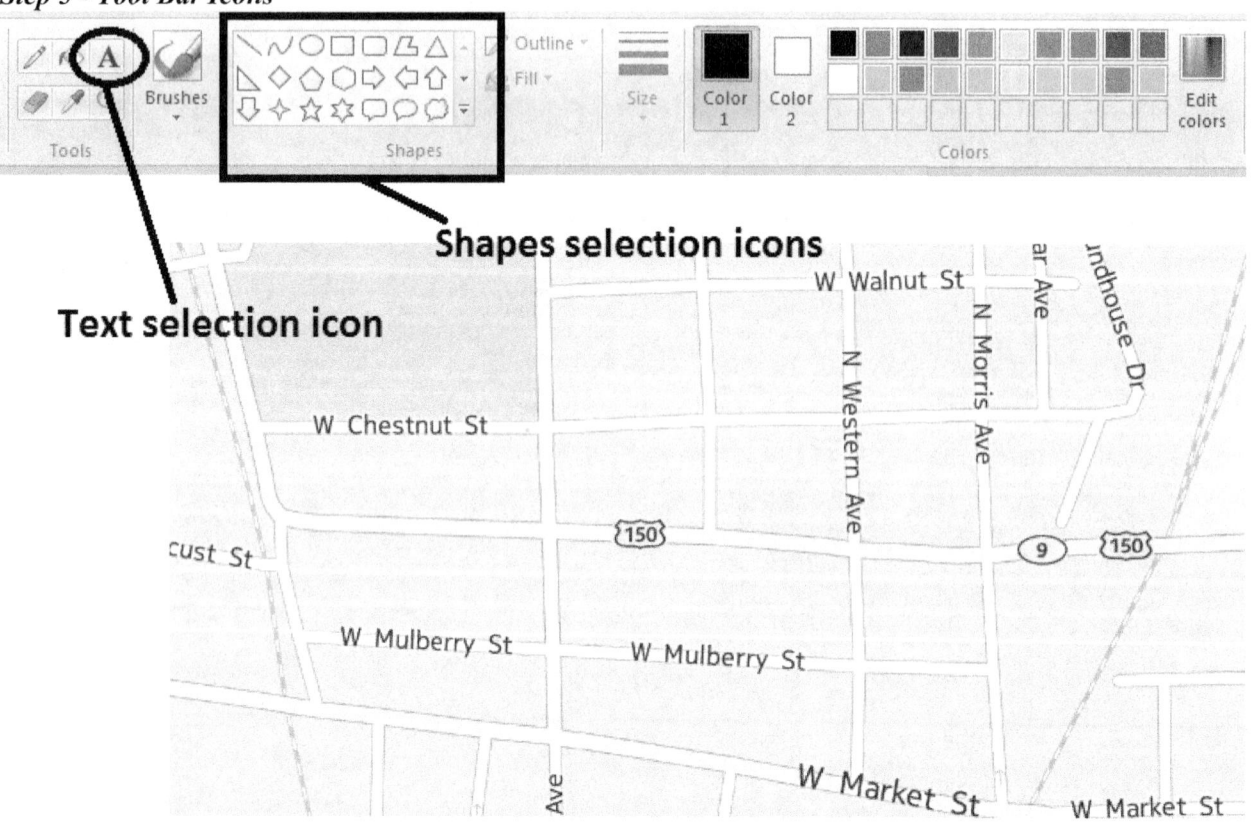

80

Timelines in Family Histories

Use timelines. They will give you a basic outline for your family history and I guarantee that they will lead you to be more successful in your genealogy research and will make your family history research more complete and exciting.

They are a tool when doing research but I also include them in my family histories. They are such a great visual tool for the written histories because they help family members understand the movements of the family. I use two formats to display timelines. One format is a map and the other format is as a list of events in chronological order.

My summaries focus on the individuals. The timelines allow me to capture the total picture of the family's arrival in America or the migration of some pioneer family branches across America from the east coast to the west coast. Timelines are also an important tool to organize and assess the tremendous amount of information I have uncovered for my family history.

- The timeline is a visual tool that should show events in chronological order. It can show gaps and inconsistencies in the information that you have found for your family history. Identifying gaps will help resolve data conflicts and show you where you should direct your next efforts at gathering information.

- A family timeline showing locations and dates will indicate the movements of the family and point to possible new locations to look for documents. More documents can be found from these clues and thus fill in more of the gaps. Also the information found in these new documents can point to more areas to look for family history. This will help explain the what, where and when of some of the events.

- Timelines should list all direct ancestors and their siblings. This will help you view the data as it relates to the family group and give you a better and more complete picture of the family. This will help explain events as they relate to the individual family members.

- Timelines can also be used to examine your family history in a historical perspective. After entering your family events in your timeline, enter various historical events that may have affected your ancestors. This will help explain the historical context of certain events in the family history and possibly show the significance of your family events.

Below is the migration map that is also a timeline showing the movement of a family across the United States. On the next page is another example of a timeline showing the relationship of the arrival of my grandparents to their siblings, cousins and friends. This is meant to explain how my grandparents arrived in Bloomington Illinois where I was born.

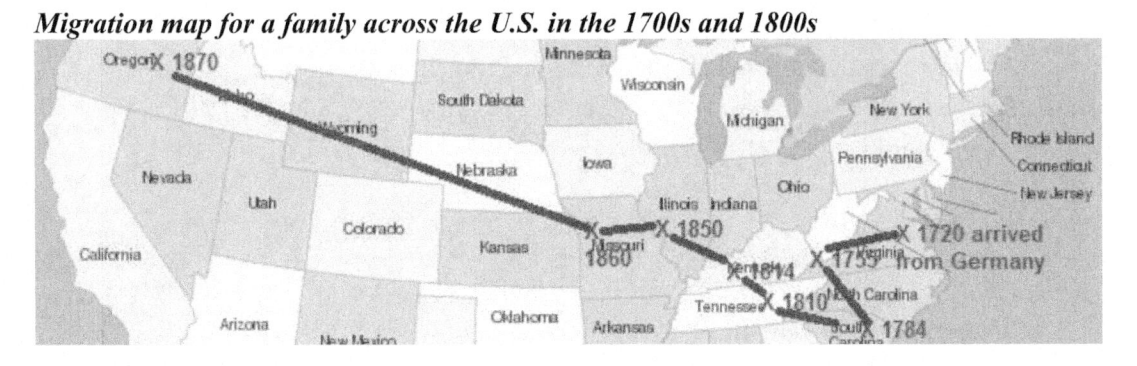

Migration map for a family across the U.S. in the 1700s and 1800s

Writing Your Family History

Here is a sample of a timeline that is a list of events. This example explains how my Polish grandparents arrived in Bloomington Illinois where I grew up.

1906 – Alex Dmochowski (cousin of Boleslaw and Steve Zuchowski)
- He arrived in Philadelphia on April 9, 1906 on SS Merion with destination of cousin J Dubinenski in Norwich, Connecticut.
- He is mentioned because he was the final destination for his cousin Boleslaw Zuchowski in 1907
- He married Rosie Choroszewicz in 1907 in Wilmington, Delaware before moving to Camden, New Jersey
- Alex and Hipolit Chmielewski helped Steve Zuchowski and Anna Chmielewski meet in Camden about 1922 which led to their marriage in 1923.

1907 – Boleslaw Zuchowski (my grandfather's brother)
- Departed Bremen with his cousin Konstanty Dmochowski
- Arrived in New York April 27, 1907 with his destination listed as his cousin Alexander Dmochowski in Norwich, Connecticut
- Moved to Bloomington, Illinois in 1909 to work at the McLean County Coal Mine
- Boleslaw married Bernice Uszcienski in November 1909 in Bloomington.
- He was the destination for his sister Marianna (1910) and brother Steve (1912)
- He returned to Poland about 1913

1910 - Marianna Zuchowski (my grandfather's sister)
- Departed Hamburg September 10, 1910
- Arrived in New York on September 27, 1910 with her destination listed as her brother Boleslaw in Bloomington, Illinois.
- She and her husband Wincenty Lapinski lived at 407 N Morris Avenue in Bloomington when their first child Helen was born in 1912.
- Returned to Poland in the early 1920s but husband Wincenty, daughter Helen, and son Mike returned to America. Wincenty in 1926, Helen in 1928 and Mike in 1938.

1912 - Steve Zuchowski (my grandfather)
- Departed Bremen in October 1912
- Arrived in Philadelphia on October 16, 1912 with his destination listed as his brother Boleslaw in Bloomington, Illinois

Chmielewski Family
1910 – Hipolit Chmielewski (my grandmother's brother)
- Departed Bremen, Germany on April 21, 1910
- Arrived in Philadelphia on May 3, 1910.
- His destination was his cousin Jan Sutkowski at 314 Brown Street in Philadelphia
- His passenger manifest listed that he left his mother Julia in Pierzchaly.
- He married and moved across the Delaware river to Camden, New Jersey in about 1918
- He along with his wife and children returned to Poland about 1923.

1921 - Anna Chmielewski (my grandmother)
- Departed Bremen, Germany in June 1921
- Arrived in New York on June 10, 1921 with destination listed as her brother Hipolit in Camden, New York. She left her brother Boleslaw in Przezdziecko.

Immigration, Birthplaces and Customs

Adding sections for immigration, descriptions of birthplaces and ethnic customs increases understanding of our roots. These sections can be an important part of the story of our ancestors.

Although these sections include very little specific information about our ancestors, the general information that is included does help us understand their lives before their immigration to America. Reviewing the political, social and economic history will add insight into their lives and gives possible reasons for their immigration.

Most families do not have oral history or documentation that explain why their ancestors immigrated. General sources such as histories may give us a picture of where our ancestors left so that we can guess at what their lives were like and why they left. Even if some oral history has been passed down, studying history can help determine how to verify the accuracy of the family stories. Reviewing the history of the country gives some general insight but finding a history of the specific county or village where they left gives insights that should apply to our ancestors more closely. I have used books from the library and articles on Wikipedia.org to study the history of the country but have relied on the internet to search for histories of counties and villages. County websites normally have a page for their history and they may also have a gallery of vintage pictures of the village and area. Googling for the history of the county, town or village may also yield useful information and pictures.

Background information for various ethnic groups can add insights to the picture of the immigrants' life where we have not been able to find any specific documents. I used selective history books for specific countries and ethnic groups to gain some of this information. I have also found some of these histories on genealogy websites for various groups.

Review any information that you find about the county and area for problems that may have caused political, religious or economic reasons to leave. Examples that I found that may have affected my ancestors include the following:
- A fungus that destroyed vineyards in Slovenia
- Prussia forcing Polish farmers off their lands and selling the land to Germans
- Prussia forcing the Poles to use German in their schools
- Lack of industrialization in Russian and Austrian controlled areas of Poland causing many unemployed farmers to emigrate.
- In heritance laws that limited ownership of the farm to only the oldest sons. This forced many of the younger children to emigrate.
- Religious persecution of the Puritans, Huguenots and Scots-Irish
- The Irish Potato Famine

Gathering this information will require studying history to give us a picture of their possible lives in the "old country" and to find clues that can give us possible reasons for their immigration.

Writing Your Family History

A sample of a portion of a page describing the immigration of my Polish ancestors

My grandparents, Steve Zuchowski and Anna Chmielewski, were born in an area of Poland that was south of Lomza and had been partitioned (annexed) by Russia in 1795. Their villages were located about four miles from one another and were about 60 miles northeast of Warsaw. The lands that their families farmed had been part of old manor estates which by 1880 had been sub-divided into many smaller farms. Although both were descendants of the Polish nobles who had owned large estates, the small size of the farms that their fathers owned in early the 1900s made it difficult to support their families. Economic problems in the Lomza district forced many who did not own land to emigrate. Since Steve had two older brothers, he could not hope to own land and emigration was the option he chose. He was 19 when he left and even though he was still required to serve in the Russia military. Was his military service requirement another reason why he left and did he have to sneak across the border with Germany? Anna also had older brothers and she emigrated as a single woman in 1921 at age 21. I asked her what life was like for her during WW I and she shrugged her shoulders and said "they survived." The number of immigrants from the Lomza district ranks in the top three areas of immigration from Poland to America.

The following pages describe the emigration of my grandparents Steve Zuchowski and Anna Chmielewski plus other members of their families and some of their friends.

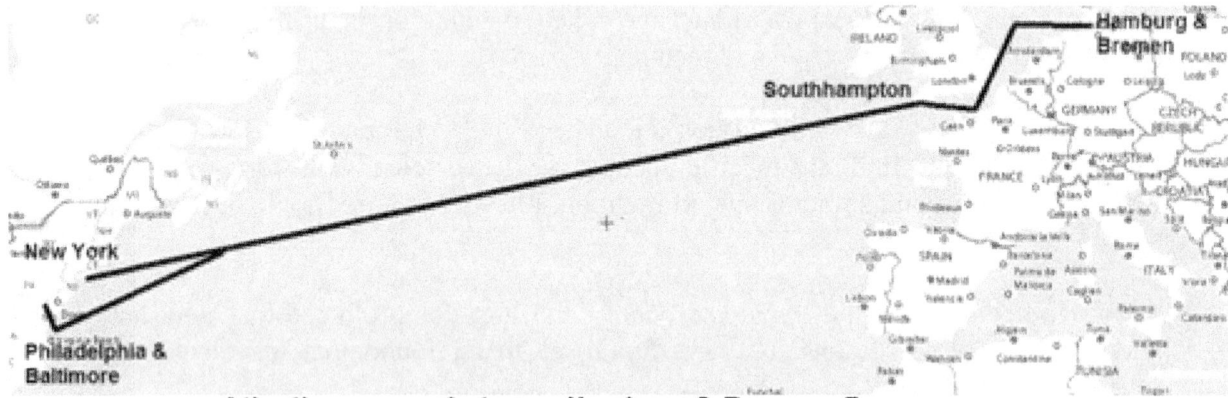

Atlantic passage between Hamburg & Bremen, Germany to New York, Philadelphia or Baltimore

Beyond the Basics

Below is a the first page for the section of my family history for The Polish Birthplaces of my Ancestors

Anna Chmielewski – Born in Przezdziecko-Pierzchaly and baptized in Andrzejewo, Russia (now Poland). Her mother was born in Zaluski-Lipniewo

Steve Zuchowski – Born in Dmochy Kudly, baptized in Czyzew, Russia (now Poland). His mother was also born in Dmochy Kudly and his father was born in Dmochy Wochy.

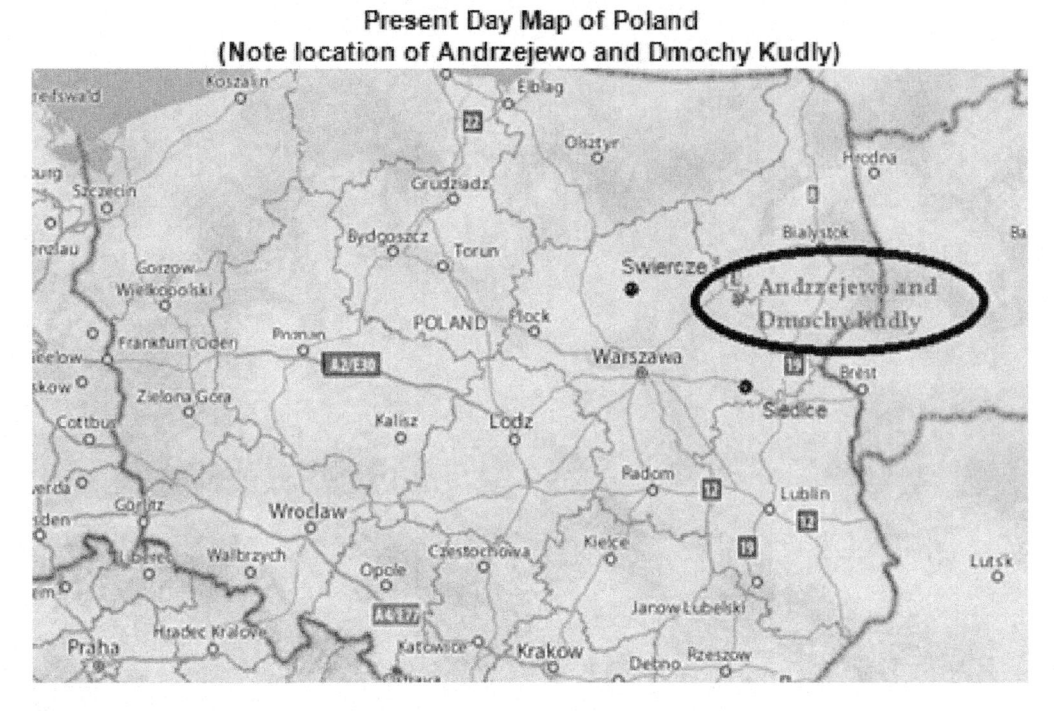

Present Day Map of Poland
(Note location of Andrzejewo and Dmochy Kudly)

Przezdziecko Pierzchaly - (birthplace of Anna Chmielewska Zuchowski and her Chmielewski ancestors)
Przezdziecko-Pierzchaly is a small farm village about 3 miles north of Andrzejewo and it is located next to the town of Przezdziecko-Jachy and along the banks of the river Little Brok. Nearby is a very old cemetery and according to an old legend the village stands near the site of a small ancient pagan stone temple. In 1827 the village had 7 homes and 58 people. This was the family home of my grandmother Anna Chmielewski and her parents – Alexander Chmielewski and Julia Zaluska. Church records from 1860 to 1865 listed the names of nine families that lived in Przezdziecko-Pierzchaly – Chmielewski, Jablonowski, Kierzysicizki, Kruszewski, Misztalowski, Przedriezski, Sutkowski, Wolinski and Zaluska.

Przezdziecko was an "okolica szlachecka" (a noble manor estate) that was located on the lands along the banks of the Maly Brok (Little Brok) river and just north of Andrzejewo, Poland. In the early 1400s, the Prince of Mazoniecki (Mazonia) gave frontier lands to various Polish knights to increase the security along his borders. The knights became feudal lords over the lands and they became noblemen with political power. In return the knights were to attract settlers to develop the lands for income plus defend the border against invasion from the Prince's enemies. Early owners of Przezdziecko were the nobles of the Przezdziecki and Drogaoszewski families. The manor home was located near present day Przezdziecko-Drogoszewo

Summary

Adding pictures to my summaries seem to bring my ancestors back to life. It is easier to visual their everyday lives when I see them with other family members and pictures of their homes. Maps showing the locations of their homes and the path of any immigration the family took also added to my understanding of their lives.

Sections describing the immigration of my ancestors, their birthplaces and their customs added the pieces for my understanding my heritage and roots.

CHAPTER SEVEN – PUBLISHING YOUR FAMILY HISTORY

Why publish your family history

Sharing your genealogy research with your family can be done very easily with a ring binder full of copies of your summaries, pictures and documents. Your family can view the pages in your ring binder when visiting or at family functions. You can also give them copies of any sections that may be of interest to them.

So why publish your family history in a bound book?

The primary reason that I began publishing my family history was to preserve what I found for future generations.

- I hope to preserve the stories, documents and pictures by distributing multiple copies of them in a bound book. Note that a bound book would probably be saved where as a ring binder or folders and documents may be torn out. Multiple copies may insure more copies would survive over time.
- A secondary reason is that by showing my research to other family members, they may remember new stories or find more pictures and documents that can be added to the pages in the history. As stated in previous pages, showing your work may refresh the memories of some members of your family and result in their sharing more stories, pictures and documents.
- Having my family history in a bound book makes it easier to donate it to local historical and genealogical libraries. This will make it available for future generations to include in their research.

Initially you may think of a published family history as a thick bound hard cover book full of boring charts, copies of documents and some pictures. This type of book was difficult and costly to publish in the past. However, today's technology makes this task much easier and economical. Also I hope that you remember that I emphasized the importance of making the focus of the family history is the stories that are found in the documents and pictures. The stories change the pages of your family history into an interesting book to read and save. It still includes those boring charts and documents but these are now secondary to the text that comes out of them. The stories begin to make your ancestors seem alive.

When should you publish your family history

Many people think that they should do the research and then after they have completed their research, they will compile the information into a book to be published. However, I believe that you should not wait until you have completed your research to start writing your family history. The reality of genealogy research is you will never be done. There will always be an unanswered question that has eluded an answer even after years of hard work on your part. As we discussed in previous chapters, writing sections of your history as you find the information is a more efficient process. Sharing portions of your research with your family members on a regular basis is also highly recommended as this will probably generate more information from them.

After the volume in your ring binder starts to build, you should consider distributing copies to your family. My decision to do this came after about seven years of research and when the amount of new information that I was finding became very small. Once I had published and distributed copies to about twenty cousins I continued to do research and making revisions to the history. I have no regrets to publishing the family history when I did because there was too much information included in the history that I wanted to preserve. I felt distributing copies to the cousins would help preserve this information. Do not be afraid that you may be missing a significant piece of information. Think of the amount and value of the information that you are saving by distributing bound copies of your history. The cost of distributing the twenty copies was about $150 which is a bargain compared to the value of the information that I gave to my cousins.

Another option to consider in making your decision to publish your work would be to have it available for a special event such as a family reunion, birthday or anniversary. Here there is more incentive to get started writing your family history and have it ready to publish by a specific date. In this situation, it is more likely that there will be pieces missing when you need to publish and the need for a later edition will be more of a reality. However, the revision now will be easier to do since the organization and bulk of the work has been done. The enthusiasm generated by many of the event participants at the event can easily make the revision efforts even easier.

Whatever course you decide to take in publishing your family history, remember that it is important to do something, and not necessarily wait until your research is finished.

How

Today, we have two options to publish our books. One is to find a commercial publisher and the other is to become our own publisher (self-publish). There are advantages to both methods as there are problems for both. However the vast majority of family histories are self published.

As my own publisher, I am responsible for not only preparing the content as the author but also understand the printer's requirement for a print ready manuscript. The publisher will also make decisions on the page size, quality of paper, hardcover or soft cover. I will decide on the printer, distribution and marketing options. Do I use a short run printing company or print-on-demand. All of these decisions affect the cost of each book and the time needed to publish and print the book.

You may have seen family histories that were done years old that were hardbound and contained many charts, a few biographical sketches of some ancestors and some pictures. These books were difficult and costly to publish. In the past, an author found a company to publish their family history using mail and telephone. They then had to supply the content that consisted of pages that they typed and copies of pictures and documents. The author had to pay a setup charge which today is $500 to $1000. Next to consider was the minimum order quantity which was about 50 and the printing costs which amount to about $25 to $50 per book. The entire order was shipped to the author and then was distributed to the family. Another concern is who paid for the setup and printing of the book. Did one person pay for everything and give the book to the family or did the family share the cost? If some of the family agreed to share the cost, was there enough to match the minimum order quantity? As you can see printing a family history was a complicated and challenging process.

Today's technology makes this process much simpler and more economical.

Publishing

Today's publishing options offer Print-on-Demand and eBooks as sources for the publishing and distribution of family histories and genealogies. Few traditional publishers will even consider paying to publish a genealogical publication unless it had a broad appeal. Their printing process was to print thousands of copies at one time. Running the small quantities needed for family histories was not cost effective. Only a few publishers would print copies of family histories after they charged the setup fees and a minimum printing fee.

Print-on-Demand

Print-on-demand (POD) may be the answer to the small quantities needed for family histories. I have published seven family histories using this format. POD uses electronic book publishing printing systems that can print one book or a hundred at economical costs. The content of the book can also be easily updated by just uploading a new file to the printer. As part of the basic system, the author will do the editing and proof reading although some companies offer these professional services at an additional cost. The main drawback is that these systems can only use the soft cover glued binding. Here are a few of the online services that will print one or more books for various pricing alternatives:

- Blurb (website: Blurb.com) – no setup, offers soft cover and hardbound, pricing based on page size, number of pages, binding, and paper options, minimum order quantity is one but larger quantities receive discounts. The cost can be calculated on their website.
- Booklocker (website: Booklocker.com) – No setup, $35 fee to proof print, annual $18 hosting fee.
- Createspace (website: Createspace.com) – No longer available. Createspace was merged into Kindle Direct Publishing (KDP).
- Kindle Direct Publishing (website: KDP.Amazon.com) – No setup fee, minimum order of one, no discount on large quantity orders but has lowest cost printing.
- Lulu (website: Lulu.com) No setup fee, minimum order of one.
- Infinity Publishing (website: InfinityPublishing.com) – cost of soft cover package $599 & hardcover $849
- Iuniverse (website: Iuniverse.com) – print on demand but has setup cost $849

The advantage of having a print-on-demand publisher is:
1. You do not to have raise money from relatives to buy the books
2. You can reorder one copy or any quantity as interest grows within your family to read about your ancestors.
3. Relatives can order their copies directly from publisher.
4. The books are less expensive than small run publishing and are very economical to setup and print
5. Many POD publishers allow you to keep the rights to your book

If you are determined to have a hardbound book, there are several genealogical publishing companies that will produce a hardbound book from your file at considerably more cost of each book. Here are some suggested sources:
- Stories To Tell (website at www.storiestotellbooks.com)
- Creative Continuum (website at creativecontinuum.com)
- Higginson Book Company (website at www.higginsonbooks.com)
- Family Heritage Publishers (website at www.familyheritagepublishers.com)
- Family History Publishers, Inc. (website at www.familyhistorypublisher.com)
- Infinity Publishing (website at InfinityPublishing.com
- Lulu (website at www.lulu.com)

eBooks

Another facet of modern technology to be considered for publishing your family history is the eBook. The use of eReaders such as the Kindle and the Apple iPad by a growing number people makes this format an alternative that should be considered. EBook publishing is similar to traditional publishing except for the final printing and binding. The author also needs to develop editing skills to adapt the format of the book to fit the eBook format. This generally requires adjusting the page size and positioning of the images to fit the eReader screen sizes. One advantage of publishing in eBook format is that the content can be updated at any time and copies can easily be distributed. One disadvantage of using an eBook publisher is the size limitations that some have. Since family histories may contain many images such as documents and family pictures, the required memory size may be too large for some publishers. Too large of a document may affect the download speed to an eReader and may affect its readability if the reader's memory is small. In testing this format, I have found some documents such as census of passenger records are difficult to read on an eReader. Some suggestions for eBook publishers are:

- Amazon Kindle Direct Publishing
- Barnes and Noble's Pubit
- Lulu
- Smashbooks
- Bookbaby

Another option is to publish in both formats and a few of the publishers listed above will publish in both a print version and an eBook.

Self-publishing a print book and an eBook are both easy using most of the self publishing websites. You choose a size for your book, format your Word manuscript to fit that size, turn your Word doc into a PDF, create some cover art in Photoshop, turn that into a PDF, and upload it all to the self-publisher of your choice and get a book proof back within a couple of weeks. If you need to make changes, you can then make changes and upload a new PDF. Both KDP and Lulu seem to be user friendly and have good instructions for the self publishers.

My POD experience

I initially used Createspace.com which is a division of Amazon.com. It was strictly POD and offered quality printing of my books at a very reasonable price. However, Amazon merged their services into Kindle Direct Publishing and their new policies made it difficult to keep family histories private. On KDP all books have to be available for sale on Amazon.com and the private website for individual books was discontinued. Due to these changes, I now publish my family histories on Lulu.com because they provide a private website and authors can hold back books from public distribution. These two features will protect the privacy of my family histories and allow me to keep control of their distribution. The free webpage for each book allows relatives to order additional copies without contacting me. Lulu offers both softcover and hardcover bindings. Lulu also offers free ISBN numbers and has an online cover creator with templates for professional looking covers. The cost of printing at Lulu is slightly higher ($1-3 per copy) than KDP but solving the privacy issues makes Lulu more attractive printer for my family histories. For additional fees, they also offer professional services for cover design, editing and marketing.

I have published over fifteen family histories using Createspace and have now moved them to Lulu.com for future distribution. I want to describe the process so you have an idea of what to expect if you want to publish your family history using a print-on-demand company.

Doing the research and creating my summaries is my first step towards publishing a family history. Each book that I created was from the word document that I compiled from my summaries.

Publishing

Once I decided to publish this as a book for my family, I used the following steps:
- Merged all of my summaries into one document, organized it into a readable family history, and added index.
- I saved the document to my hard drive as a PDF
- Next, I signed into my account on Lulu.com
- Selected "Start a Project" in the left-hand menu, and select the type of project: paperback, hardcover, or eBook, but photo book and calendar is also available.
- On the next page, select the type of binding and the size of the pages.
- The next page prompted me to enter the title and author
- The next page, ask to add an ISBN or none. I could add my own or seek a free SBN from Lulu.
- The next step was to unload my interior pages
- After the interior pages had uploaded, the system allowed me to review the pages for appearance.
- Next, it was time to work on the cover. I could upload a PDF of a custom cover design or use Lulu's online cover creator.
- The next step was to finish the book setup which included selecting distribution channels, pricing and adding a book description. The distribution choices are to sell in normal retail channels (Lulu, Amazon, Barnes & Noble, and others), Lulu only, direct access (private URL only), or private access.
- The price I set is cost plus a little extra amount. I usually set the price at $14.99. The extra built into the price is in case I have made a mistake in my calculations.
- Next, I order a proof copy to do a final edit for spelling, Grammar, content, appearance, and readability.
- Once I have proof read the book and made any needed changes, I would approve it for publication
- I would then place orders for my family.

Everybody who has viewed my books have enjoyed the quality and professional look of the book. Some of the quality may be due to my attention to detail but much of this is due to the system Lulu.com has setup. Lulu.com does make a complicated process as simple as possible.

Appendix B shows screen shots of the Lulu.com pages that walks you through this process.

Privacy Concerns

Another aspect of the publishing process is how private do you want to keep your family history. All of the self publishing companies are there to help independent writers produce their books to be sold to the general public. Producing books to be distributed to only family members is possible but care must be used to setup the distribution channels offered by the publishing companies. If you do not want your family history offered in retail channels such as Amazon, Barnes and Noble and other online book sellers, these channels must be turned off or deselected. Usually eBooks produced by one of the online publishing companies can only be distributed through a retail channel and you may not want to publish online using this format. However, if a relative wants a copy for their eReader, you can format a copy in the correct size for their reader, save it as a PDF and then send them the copy. Most eReaders have software to read a PDF file.

Another privacy concern for your published work would be listing living people in the charts that you include. I avoid including generations that include my children and my grandchildren. I also do not include birth information for people in my generation.

More points to consider when publishing your family history

- Do not overly edit the words that your relatives used in telling their stories. Care must be taken that your editing not change the intended meaning of your relative's words. Their style and grammar may best describe the person or situation of the story.
- Get permission from living persons before you write anything about them.
- Don't let your history become a list of names, dates and places. Include stories and background information to bring the history to life.
- Use general historical information about the place and time of your ancestors to put their lives into historical perspective.
- Try to present your information to show the challenges your ancestors faced and help your readers to empathize with them.
- Before you include sensitive material in your writing, discuss it with anyone you think may be concerned or affected by the material.
- If you find scandals or embarrassing information in your research you should consider how it affects your family history. Is it about your ancestor or one of their siblings? Should you include it in your history or not? Remember that you found the information and someone in the future will also find it. Including the information in a sensitive manner now may be better than omitting it from the family history that you share with family.

Final Thoughts

CHAPTER EIGHT – MY FINAL THOUGHTS ON WRITING YOUR FAMILY HISTORY

Writing an accurate family history is a challenging task. I recommend that if you want to accomplish this, you should concentrate on doing quality research in the beginning. As you find information compile your research onto readable documents for each individual. These I call summaries and I use them as reference tools to help me with my research and the summaries are also great to share information with your family members.

When I started my research, I could not envision myself as a writer and I could not believe that I had the organizational and writing skills to do such an important writing project. Somehow my research methods produced biographical narratives in small sections that could be combined to produce family histories that are being enjoyed by many family members.

The key was focusing on doing the research and writing summaries to share with family members. These small pieces could eventually be combined into a great family history. Without my summaries I could not have written my family histories.

The summaries that were the basis for the family history were initially written to help with my research and to help share the information with my family. As I connected with family members, groups of summaries were merged together to share information about their ancestors. Over time the merged groups of summaries were combined and organized in one large document that became the family history that was published and distributed to the family members. As you can see the family history came together almost by accident and this method put very little pressure on me to produce such an important document.

There was a lot of work to do the research and keep the summaries updated but the final document seemed to emerge and cry out to be published. Also note that the summaries and documents could also stay in the ring binders and not be published because the ring binder will still be organized enough for someone in the future to pickup and continue your work. However, publishing your work gives the family more copies of your work and more chances that your work will survive and be available for someone in the future to continue your work.

A family history can be a great treasure to you, your family and future generations. It can help us understand our heritage both here in the U.S. and where our ancestors came from. It lets us gain knowledge and appreciation for our ancestors and their lives.

Whichever path you choose, do the work so it can be organized and saved to be used by future generations. Get the details and do the work so that it's worth saving.

Do it now!

APPENDIX A – MY FAMILY HISTORY PAGES

Here is an example of a section of one of my family histories listing the information for Julia Sirovatka and her children. She was married twice. Her first husband Josef Joza died in 1912 and she then married Frank Hlavac. She had six children with Josef and four children with Frank.

Summary of Notes for Julia Sirovatka Joza Hlavac

Julia abt 1910

Julia's birth certificate listed that she was born on December 18, 1880 at 2 Nut Court (now 1913 S Miller Street) in Chicago, Illinois to Wenzl Sirovatka and Josephine Kott.

Marriage records listed that she married Josef Joza on September 20, 1900 in Chicago, Illinois. Note that this was a civil ceremony and was performed by John C Murphy who was a Justice of the Peace.

Josef and Julia had six children - James (born in 1901), Mary (born in 1903), Julia (born in 1905), Helen (born in 1907), Josephine (born in 1910) and Karel (born in 1912). Note that Helen (d.1912) and Karel (d.1915) died as children.

The 1901 and 1905 baptismal records for son James and daughter Julia listed that the family lived at 1318 S Whipple (now 2717 S Whipple) in Chicago, Illinois.

The 1906 naturalization petition for Josef listed that the family lived at 1422 S Spaulding (now 2849 S Spaulding).

The 1910 census listed that Josef lived at 2849 S Spaulding with his wife Julia and children James, Mary, Julia, Helen and Josephine. Josef was a tailor.

Josef died at home at 2849 S Spalding on February 20, 1912 at 10 pm of lobar pneumonia

Julia married Frank Hlavac on October 14, 1914 in Chicago by a justice of the peace. They had three children – Bessie (b. 1915, Edward (b. 1917) and Ludmilla (b. 1922).

Julia with husband Josef and son James

Julia about 1920

Bessie's 1915 birth certificate listed that she was child number eight and that seven children were living. Helen would have been the child that died the five remaining Joza children and Bessie would have then totaled only 6 living not seven. Edward's birth certificate listed that he also was child number eight and that only six were alive – Helen and Karel had died. Edward's birth certificate seems to have the correct number of children and no records have been found to identify any children born prior to Bessie other than the six already listed.

Note that the 1930 census listed a second child named Josephine who was born in 1920. Also note that two pictures taken in about 1923 shows a small girl who was about age two that could be the second Josephine but in 2008 Bessie stated that there was no second child named Josephine. Also no birth or death records have been found to identify that Julia had another child.

The 1920, 1930 and 1940 census records listed that Julia lived at 2849 S Spaulding with her new husband Frank Hlavac and their two children Bessie and Edward along with Julia's children from her marriage to Josef Joza. Frank worked as a tailor.

Julia died on March 30, 1952 and Frank died on October 24, 1952.

Julia was buried in Bohemia National Cemetery in the same block of graves as children Helen, Karel and Ludmilla plus husbands Josef Joza and Anton Frank Hlavac.

2836 S Spaulding -2006

2849 S Spaulding about 1930

1930 Federal Census

House no.	Dwelling	Family	Name	Relation	Owned/Rented	Value	Radio	Farm	Sex	Race	Age	Marital
9849	23	37	Hlavac Anton	Head	O	4,000	R		M	W	60	M
			— Julia	Wife-H					F	W	55	M
			— Josephine	Daughter					F	W	20	S
			Joza Bessie	Daughter					F	W	14	S
			— Edward	Son					M	W	12	S
			— Josephine	Daughter					F	W	10	S
		38	Joza James	Head	R	25	R		M	W	29	M
			— Anna	Wife-H					F	W	25	M
			— Evelyn	Daughter					F	W	6	S
		39	Burkhart Gilbert	Head	R	25	R		M	W	30	M
			— Mae	Wife-H					F	W	25	M

Birth Certificate Julia Sirovatka December 18, 1880

RETURN OF A BIRTH.

No. 15032

State of Illinois, Cook County. STATE BOARD OF HEALTH.

1. *Full Name of Child (if any): July Josefin Sirovatka
2. Sex: G   Race or Color (if not of the white race): —
3. Number of Child of this Mother: 3
4. Date of this Birth: 12/18 1880
5. †Place of Birth: No. 21 West Court Street, 6 Ward.
6. Residence of Mother: "
7. Nationality: Bohem.   Place of Birth: Age of:
   a. Father: 35 y
   b. Mother: 30
8. Full Name of Mother: Josefin Sirovatka
9. Maiden Name of Mother: Hot
10. Full Name of Father: Wenzl Sirovatka
11. Occupation of ": Laborer
12. Name and address of other Attendants, if any:

Dated 187_.   Returned by: M. Keier, M.D./Midwife
Residence: 287 W. 20 St.

Writing Your Family History

Marriage Certificate – Josef Joza & Julia Sirovatka
September 24, 1900

Marriage Certificate – Julia Sirovatka Joza & Frank Hlavac
October 14, 1914

My Family History Pages

Julia Sirovatka Joza Hlavac
Died March 30, 1952
Burial at
Bohemian National Cemetery
In Block 4
5255 NORTH PULASKI RD.
CHICAGO, ILLINOIS 60630

Gate House Entrance for Bohemian National Cemetery

Julia's Grave Marker

Family Grave Marker that includes Josef Joza

Aerial view of Bohemian National Cemetery

Map of Bohemian National Cemetery

Obituary for Julia Syrovatka Joza Hlavac - panel

From Denni Hlasatel Monday March 31, 1952

OZNÁMENÍ ÚMRTÍ
JULIA HLAVÁČ

býv. JOZA — obydlí 2849 již. Spaulding Avenue

zemřela v neděli, dne 30. března 1952, ve 3:45 hod. odpoledne, u věku 72 roků. Narozena byla v Chicagu. Byla členkyní Sboru Spravedlnost čís. 141 J.Č.D.aP., Sboru Karolina Světlá čís. 11 Ú.J.Č.A.Ž. a Klubu Palmový Lupen. Pohřeb drahé zesnulé konati se bude ve středu, dne 2. dubna 1952, v 10 hodin dopoledne, z kaple pohřebního ústavu John T. Chrástka, 3440 záp. 26. ulice, na Český Národní hřbitov. — Zanechává zde:

FRANK HLAVÁČ, truchlící manžel; JAMES JOZA a EDW. HLAVÁČ, synové; MARY BERKHOUT, JULIA ROKOS, JOSEPHINE PATRICK a BESSIE HLAVÁČ, dcery; ANNA JOZA a HARRIETTE HLAVÁČ, snachy; GILBERT BERKHOUT, JOHN ROKOS a FRANK PATRICK, zeťové; sedm vnoučat, jedno pravnouče, švakři, švakrové a ostatní přátelé.

Další informace sdělí pohřební ústav John T. Chrástka, BIshop 7-9802, OLympic 2-1023.
31x2

Obituary for Frank Hlavac - panel
From Denni Hlasatel Saturday October 25, 1952

OZNÁMENÍ ÚMRTÍ
FRANK HLAVÁČ

manžel zesnulé JULIA HLAVÁČ, obydlí: 2849 South Spaulding Avenue,

zemřel v pátek, dne 24. října 1952, v 11:40 hod. ráno u věku 81 roků. Narozen byl v Třeboni v Čechách a v této zemi žil 60 roků. Byl členem sboru Vodňany č. 33, Ben Hur. Pohřeb drahého zesnulého konati se bude v pondělí, dne 27. října 1952, v 1:30 hod. odpol., z kaple pohřebního ústavu John T. Chrástka, 3440 West 26th St., na Český Národní hřbitov. — Zanechává zde:

EDWARD HLAVÁČ a JAMES JOZA, synové; BESSIE HLAVÁČ, MARY BERKHOUT, JULIA ROKOS a JOSEPHINE PATRICK, dcery; HARRIETT HLAVÁČ a ANNA JOZA, snachy; GILBERT BERKHOUT, JOHN ROKOS, FRANK PATRICK, zeťové; 7 vnoučat, 1 pravnouče a ostatní přátelé.

Další informace sdělí pohřební ústav John T. Chrástka, telefony BIshop 7-9802 anebo OLympic 2-1023.
25x2

Summary of Julia's Nine Children

James Joza

- Born on August 29, 1901 to Josef Joza and Julia Sirovatka.
- Baptized on September 8, 1901 at St Ludmilla's Church in Chicago, Illinois by Rev Mat Farnik with Carl and Marie Fink as sponsors
- James married Anna Marie Maruna about 1923 and they had two children - daughters (Evelyn – born May 15, 1924 and Arlene – born November 29, 1931)
- Anna was born on February 12, 1902 in Chicago to Joseph Maruna and Mary Poduska who were born in Bohemia.
- The 1930 census indicated that James and Anna lived at 2929 S Spaulding Avenue with daughter Evelyn in one of the apartments above his mother. His occupation was listed as foreman at a millinery factory.
- Family oral history and pictures indicates that James later owned a candy store.
- Nephew XXXX XXXXX remembers that his Uncle Jimmy worked as a switchman for the railroad from a shack along the railroad tracks on 31st street next to the Cook County jail.
- Daughter Evelyn married Frank Klecan and they had one daughter Nancy (b. 1949). Evelyn later married Frank Martin.
- Daughter Arlene married XXXXXX on April 11, 1955 and they had five children.
- James died in July, 1968 and was buried at Bohemian National Cemetery.
- Anna died in May 1987 in LaGrange Park, Illinois and was buried at Bohemian National Cemetery.

Birth Certificate from Cook County for James

Writing Your Family History

Baptismal Register at St Lumilla's Church for James

Numerus currens	Nomen Infantis	Tempus Nativitatis Dies	Mensis	Annus	Tempus Baptismi Dies	Mensis	Annus	Residentia	Nomen Patris	Parentum Matris
259	Emily	3	9	1901	7	9	1901		Wenc Krbec	Anna Janda
260	Edith	23	8	1901	7	9	1901		Rudolph Janda	Marie Kotiba
261	Wenceslas	29	8	1901	8	9	1901		Joseph Joza	Julia Sirovatka
262	Rudolph	31	8	1901	8	9	1901		John Beranek	Josephine Kolar
263	Francis	27	8	1901	8	9	1901		Frank Dolezal	Marie Divis
264	William	25	8	1901	8	9	1901		Thomas Chmelik	Agnes Cejka
265	Charles	19	8	1901	8	9	1901		Charles Siedler	

Obituary for James Joza
   Chicago Tribune (IL) - January 04, 1968
   James J. Joza, beloved husband of Anna; fond father of Evelyn [Frank] Klecan and Arlene [Ralph] Garcia; grandfather of five; brother of Mary Berkhout, Julia Rokos, Bessie Hlavac, and Edward [Harriet] Hlavac. Services Friday, Jan. 5, 10 a.m., at John T. Chrastka Memorial cemetery.

Mary Joza

- Born on April 7, 1903 to Josef Joza and Julia Sirovatka.
- Baptized on April 26, 1904 at St Ludmilla's Church in Chicago, Illinois by Rev Mat Farnik with Carl and Marie Fink as sponsors
- Married Gilbert Berkhout in 1925 and they did not have any children.
- On the marriage register Gilbert's occupation was listed as a cigar maker and Mary's occupation was a decorator.
- Gilbert was born in the Netherlands (probably Roterdam) on September 9, 1899 to Jacob "James" Berkhout and Cora Van Osten. He was one of their eight children. However, four children had died prior to 1910 and Gilbert's mother died between 1910 and 1920.
- The 1910 and 1920 census listed that Gilbert and his family lived in Grand Rapids, Michigan and all worked making cigars for their father's business.
- The 1930 census listed that Gilbert and Mary had moved to Chicago, Illinois and lived in an apartment above Mary's mother. Gilbert worked as a clerk in a dry goods store plus Mary worked as a clerk in a millinery shop.
- Nephew Terry Hlavac remembers that Uncle Gil worked as a switchman for the railroad in the tower on 29th and Kedzie right around the corner from where Gil and Mary lived.
- Gil died on 02 Jan 1964 in Chicago and was buried at Bohemian National Cemetery.
- Mary died in August, 1974 and is buried in Bohemian National Cemetery.

Obituary for Mary J. Berkhout, nee Joza
Chicago Tribune (IL) - August 31, 1974
   Mary J. Berkhout, nee Joza, beloved wife of the late Gilbert Berkhout; dear sister of Julia (the late John) Rokos, Bessie, Edward (Harriet) Hlavac, the late James (Anna) Joza and Josephine (Frank) Patrick; nieces, nephews, great-nieces and nephews and one great-great-nephew. Services Saturday, Aug. 31, 1 p.m., from Noworul Memorial Chapels, 2658 S. Central Park Av. Interment Bohemian National Cemetery.

My Family History Pages

Baptismal Register at St Lumilla's Church for Mary

Birth Certificate from Cook County for Mary

Marriage Register for Mary Joza and Gilbert Berkhout Line 2130

Julia Joza

- Born on March 26,1905 to Josef Joza and Julia Sirovatka.
- Baptized on March 26, 1905 at St Ludmilla's Church in Chicago, Illinois by Rev Frank Bobel with Carl and Marie Fink as sponsors
- Married John Rokos in 1928
- The 1930 census listed that they were living in one of the apartments above John's parents and John was working as a labor in a shop.
- Children - they had one daughter (Mildred – born June 6, 1933, died in 1993, did not marry)
- John died on January 2, 1965 and was buried at Bohemian National Cemetery.
- Died on March 31, 1991 and was buried at Bohemian National Cemetery.

Baptismal Register at St Lumilla's Church for Julia Joza

Birth Certificate for Julia Joza

My Family History Pages

Helen Joza

- Born on June 2, 1907 to Josef Joza and Julia Sirovatka.
- Baptized on June 20, 1907 at St Ludmilla's Church in Chicago, Illinois by Rev Frank Bobel with Carl and Marie Fink as sponsors
- Died at age 5 on October 13,1912 of spinal meningitis and was buried in Bohemian National Cemetery with parents.

Baptismal Register at St Lumilla's Church for Helen Joza

Birth Certificate from Cook County for Helene

Writing Your Family History

Death Certificate for Helen Joza

Josephine Joza

- Born on August 1, 1910 to Josef Joza and Julia Sirovatka.
- Baptized on February 2, 1910 at St Ludmilla's Church in Chicago, Illinois by Rev Frank Bobel with Carl and Marie Fink as sponsors
- Married Frank Petrick on June 6, 1931 in St Ludmilla's Church, Chicago, Illinois
- Children - they had five children
- Died in 1964 and was buried in Transfiguration Cemetery in Wauconda, Illinois

Baptismal Register at St Lumilla's Church for Josephine

Karel (Charles) Joza

- Born on March 7, 1912 to Josef Joza and Julia Sirovatka.
- Baptized on July 23, 1912 at St Ludmilla's Church in Chicago, Illinois by Rev Frank Bobel with Carl and Marie Fink as sponsors
- Died at age 3 on November 22, 1915 on chronic nephritis and is buried in Bohemian National Cemetery with parents.

Birth Certificate for Charles Joza

Death Certificate for Karol Joza

Writing Your Family History

Bessie Hlavac
- Born on July 7, 1915 to Frank Hlavac and Julia Sirovatka.
- Baptized on September 9, 1915 at St Ludmilla's Church in Chicago, Illinois by Rev Frank Bobel with Edward and Marie Vinopal as sponsors
- 1920 & 1930 census records listed that Bessie lived at 2849 S Spaulding with her parents.
- Died December 2, 2009 in Countryside Illinois and was buried in Bohemian National cemetery with her parents.
- She never married.

Birth Certificate from Cook County for Bessie

Obituary Bessie E. Hlavac

Chicago Tribune (IL) - Sunday, December 6, 2009
Bessie E. Hlavac , age 94, of Countryside, beloved aunt of Terry Hlavac , Evelyn Martin, Arlene Garcia, Theresa Weinberg, Susan Szabados and Joanne Mayfield; loving great-aunt to many.

Ms. Hlavac was a member of the Pioneer's Club at Western Electric. Following her retirement she served as a volunteer at LaGrange Memorial Hospital for 22 years, logging 10,000 hours of service. Ms. Hlavac was also a member of the CSA Lodge.

Visitation 3 to 9 p.m., Monday, at Hallowell & James Funeral Home, 1025 W. 55th St., Countryside, where Funeral Service will be held 11 a.m., Tuesday. Interment Bohemian National Cemetery. In lieu of flowers, memorials to St. Thomas Hospice appreciated. Funeral info 708-352-6500.

Edward Hlavac to Frank Hlavac and Julia Sirovatka.
- Born on July 14, 1917
- The 1920 and 1930 Federal Census records listed that Edward lived at 2849 S Spaulding in Chicago with his parents.
- Married Harriet Marie Hanson on April 28, 1945
- Children - one son Terry
- Edward died on January 14, 1993

Birth Certificate for Edward Hlavac

Writing Your Family History

Ludmilla Hlavac to Frank Hlavac and Julia Sirovatka.
- Born on January 17, 1922
- Died on January 19, 1922 as an infant and is buried in Bohemian National Cemetery with her parents.

Birth certificate for Ludmilla Hlavac 1922

APPENDIX B – LULU.COM EXAMPLE

My Experience
The next few pages will show you examples of the steps needed to publish on Lulu.com. I have published over fifteen family histories using Createspace and have now moved them to Lulu.com for future distribution. I want to describe the process so you have an idea of what to expect if you want to publish your family history using a print-on-demand company.

Doing the research and creating my summaries is my first step towards publishing a family history. Each book that I created was from the word document that I compiled from my summaries.

Once I decided to publish this as a book for my family, I used the following steps:
- Merged all of my summaries into one document, organized it into a readable family history, and added index.
- I saved the document to my hard drive as a PDF
- Next, I signed into my account on Lulu.com
- Selected "Start a Project" in the left-hand menu, and select the type of project: paperback, hardcover, or eBook, but photo book and calendar is also available.
- On the next page, select the type of binding and the size of the pages.
- The next page prompted me to enter the title and author
- The next page, ask to add an ISBN or none. I could add my own or seek a free SBN from Lulu.
- The next step was to unload my interior pages
- After the interior pages had uploaded, the system allowed me to review the pages for appearance.
- Next, it was time to work on the cover. I could upload a PDF of a custom cover design or use Lulu's online cover creator.
- The next step was to finish the book setup which included selecting distribution channels, pricing and adding a book description. The distribution choices are to sell in normal retail channels (Lulu, Amazon, Barnes & Noble, and others), Lulu only, direct access (private URL only), or private access.
- The price I set is cost plus a little extra amount. I usually set the price at $14.99. The extra built into the price is in case I have made a mistake in my calculations.
- Next, I order a proof copy to do a final edit for spelling, Grammar, content, appearance, and readability.
- Once I have proof read the book and made any needed changes, I would approve it for publication
- I would then place orders for my family.

Everybody who has viewed my books have enjoyed the quality and professional look of the book. Some of the quality may be due to my attention to detail but much of this is due to the system Lulu.com has setup. Lulu.com does make a complicated process as simple as possible.

The following are sample pages from Lulu.com showing the steps needed to create a new family history book:

Selected "Start a Project" in the left-hand menu, and select the type of project: Paperback Book, Hardcover Book, eBook, Photo Book, Calendar.

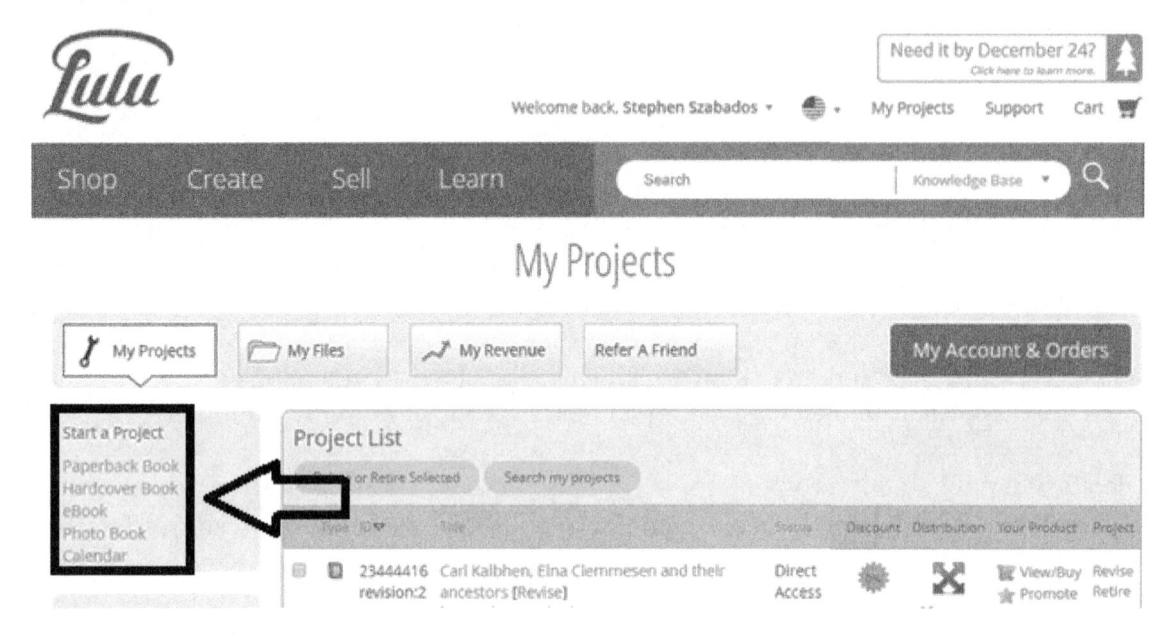

Lulu.com Example

On the next page, select the type of binding and the size of the pages. Four formats are offered: Standard Paperback, Premium Paperback, Professional Hardcover, and Photo Books and Calendar. This page shows an estimate of the cost when you type in the number of pages and then select each format. The size of the pages also affect the cost of the book but I recommend 8.5 x 11 because this larger size will increase the readability of documents such as census pages, passenger lists, and naturalization papers. An example of the webpage is shown below and on the next page.

Top Portion of beginning Book Setup Page
(Select binding and page size)

Writing Your Family History

Bottom Portion of beginning Book Setup Page
(shows a summary of your selection and text box to enter number of pages to estimate cost of book)

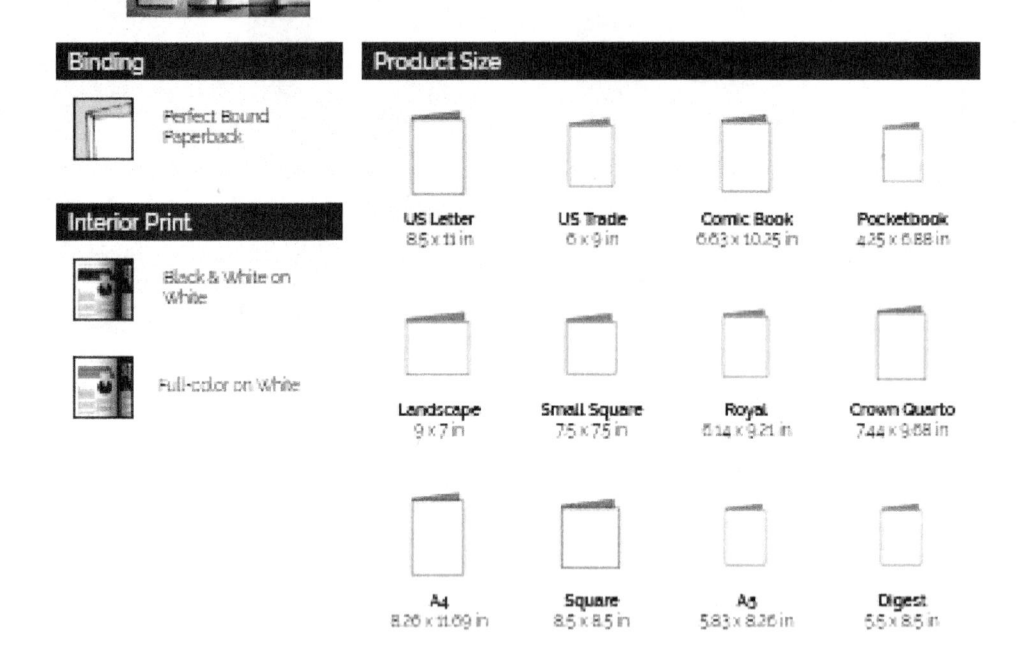

Product Line: Standard Paperback
Binding: Perfect Bound Paperback
Product Size: US Letter
Interior Color: Black & White
Paper Quality: 50#
Cover Finish: Gloss
Shipping Origin: Global

Manufacturing cost per [355] page book: $6.83
Min-Max: 84-740

↓ Download Template   Make this book ▶

+ Volume Discounts

+ Spine Measurements

Binding
Perfect Bound Paperback

Interior Print
Black & White on White

Full-color on White

Product Size

US Letter
8.5 x 11 in

US Trade
6 x 9 in

Comic Book
6.63 x 10.25 in

Pocketbook
4.25 x 6.88 in

Landscape
9 x 7 in

Small Square
7.5 x 7.5 in

Royal
6.14 x 9.21 in

Crown Quarto
7.44 x 9.68 in

A4
8.26 x 11.69 in

Square
8.5 x 8.5 in

A5
5.83 x 8.26 in

Digest
5.5 x 8.5 in

Lulu.com Example

The next page prompts to enter the title and author and select distribution choices. I recommend to select the default selection (Sell on Lulu, Amazon, Barnes & Noble, and more) at this time because this choice will allow adding an ISBN for the book which is important even if the book will be a private family history. The ISBN will make it easier to donate the book to a historical archive at a later date. Also, the distribution can be changed on the final setup page.

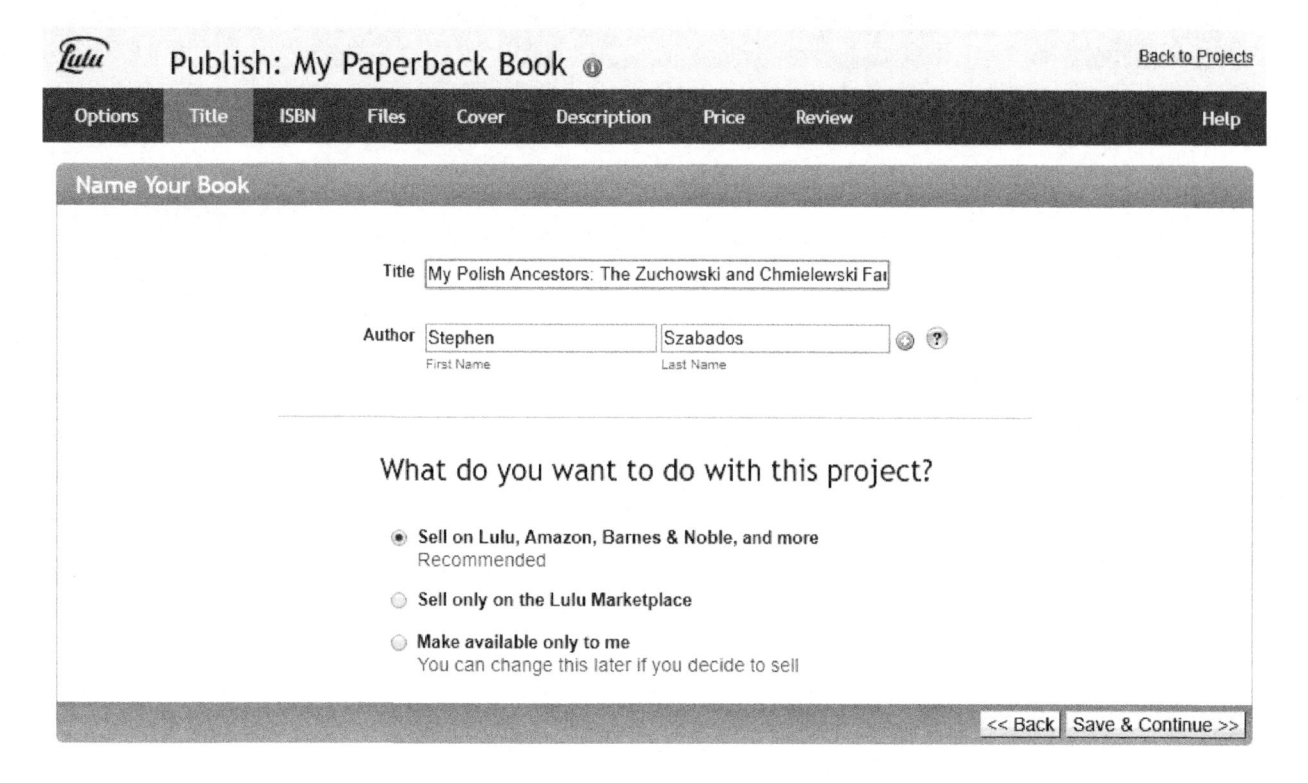

After selecting "Save & Continue," the next page allows you to add an ISBN. You can select "Get free from Lulu" or "Add an ISBN" you already own.

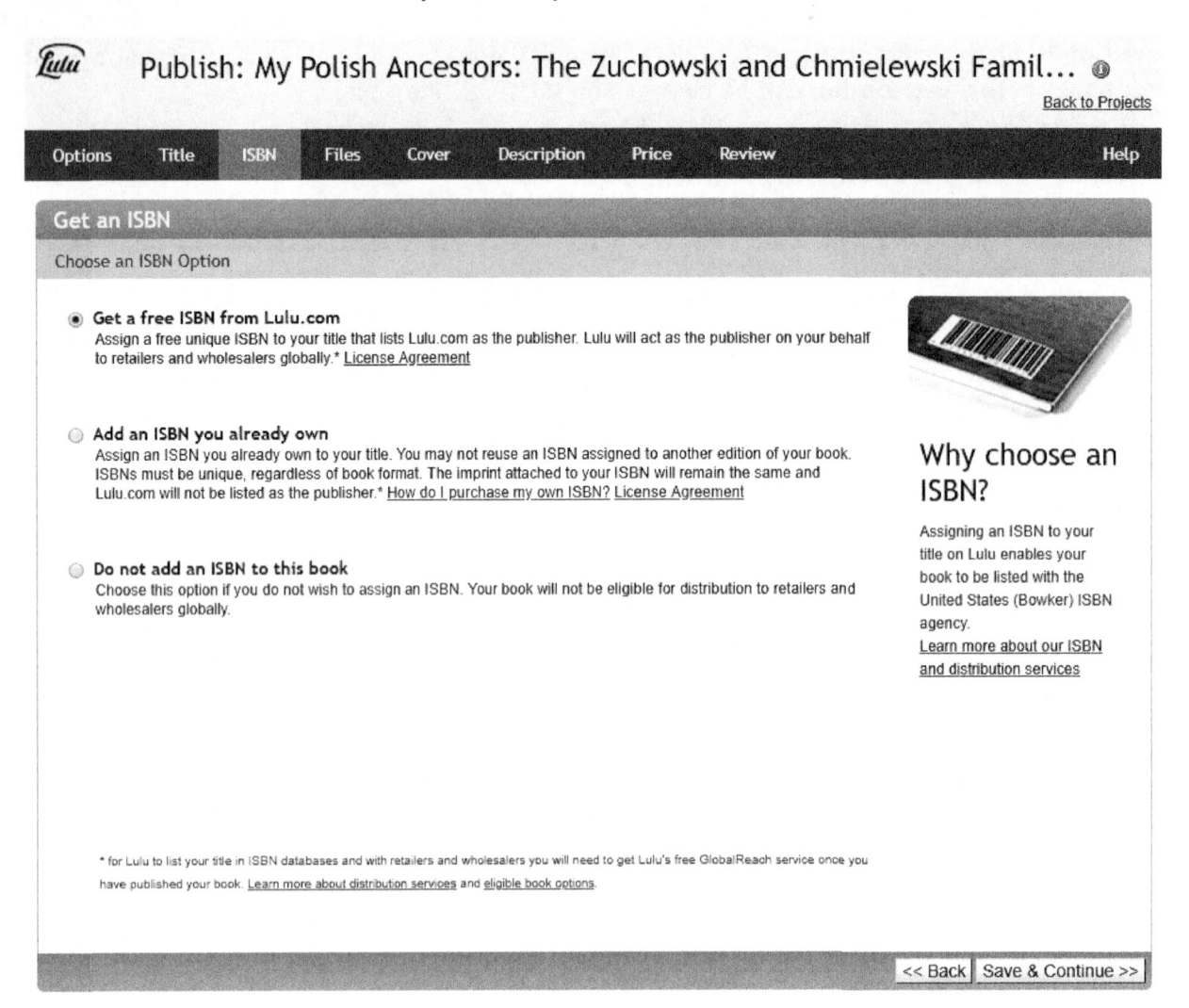

Lulu.com Example

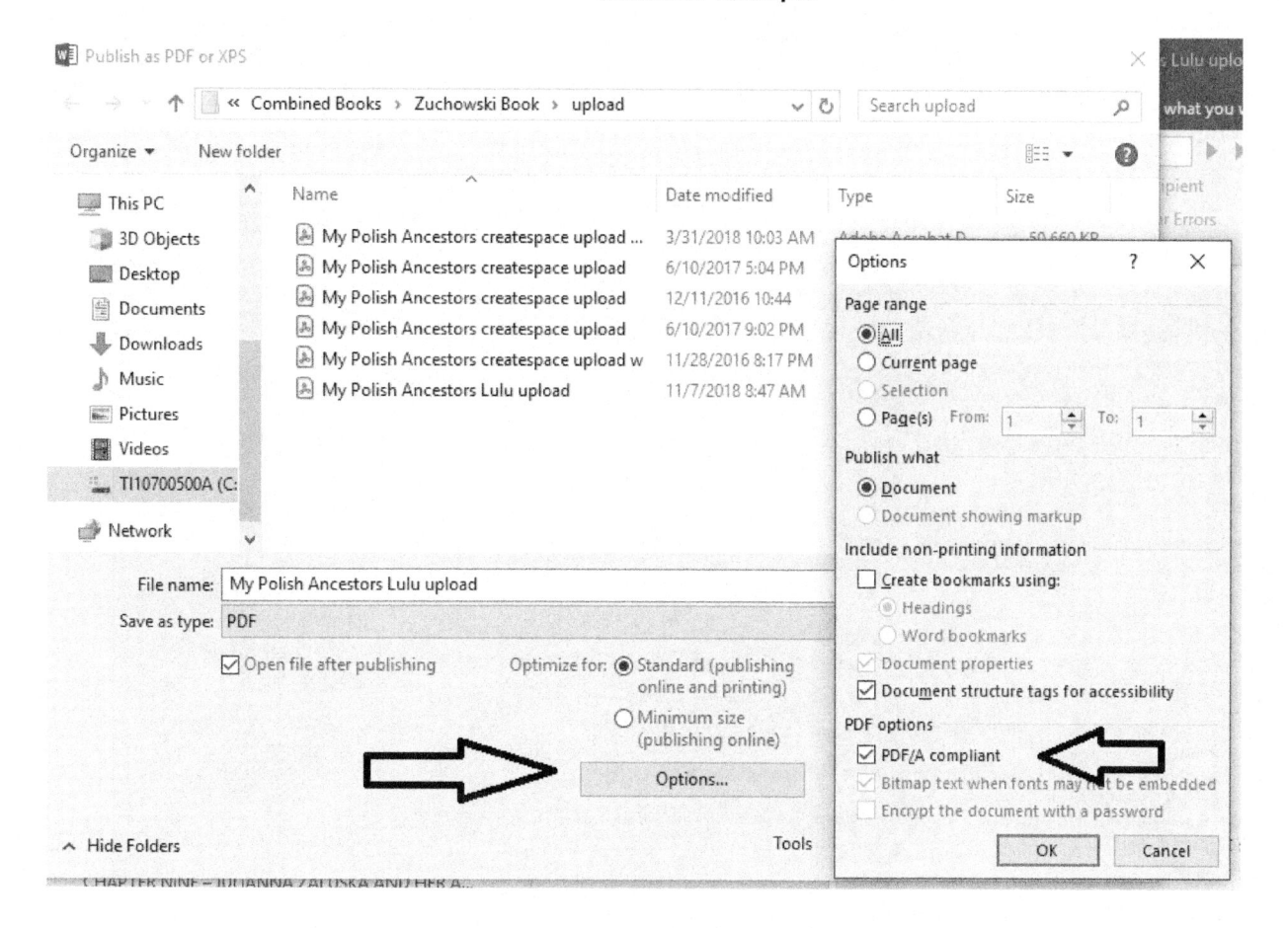

The next step is to unload the interior pages of the book. Choose the file from your hard drive and then click upload. The example below shows the "Choose File" button, the Upload button, and the upload progress bar.

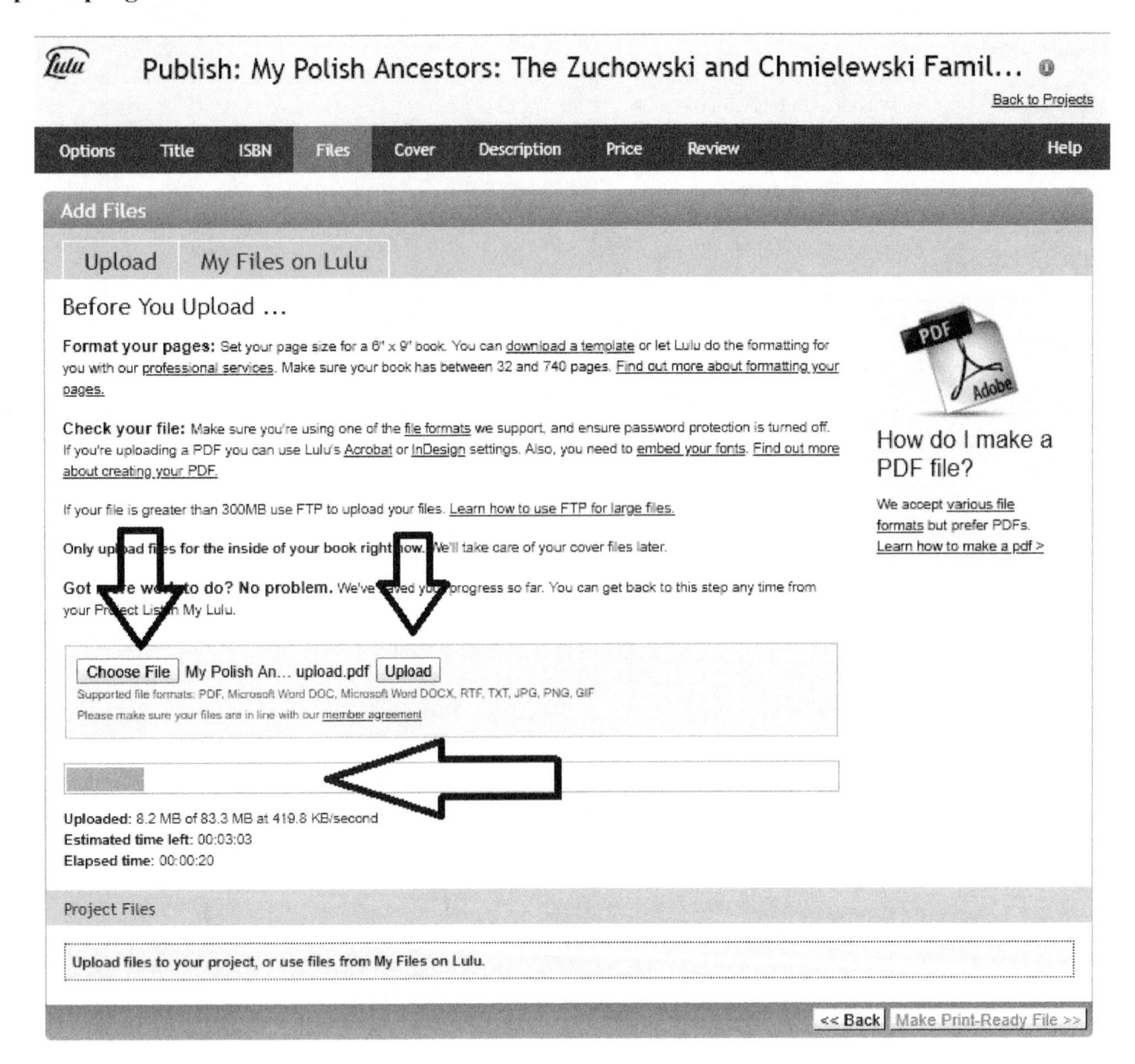

Lulu.com Example

After the upload is completed, You will have a notification at the top of the page that it is complete or there was an error that needs correction. Also the project file will be added at the bottom of the page. Next click "Make Print-Ready File" to continue. The example on the next page will show the progress of the conversion.

Example of setup page showing progress to conversion to print-ready file.

Lulu.com Example

Below is an example of conversion to print-ready file progress page after the conversion is completed. At this stage of the upload, you can download the file to review a PDF copy of the pages to make sure the appearance of the pages are as expected. Download will be PDF, make sure page layout is correct and image labels are on correct page (top or bottom of Image)

All other editing should have been done before the interior pages were uploaded.

Clicking Save & Continue will take you to the Cover creator page.

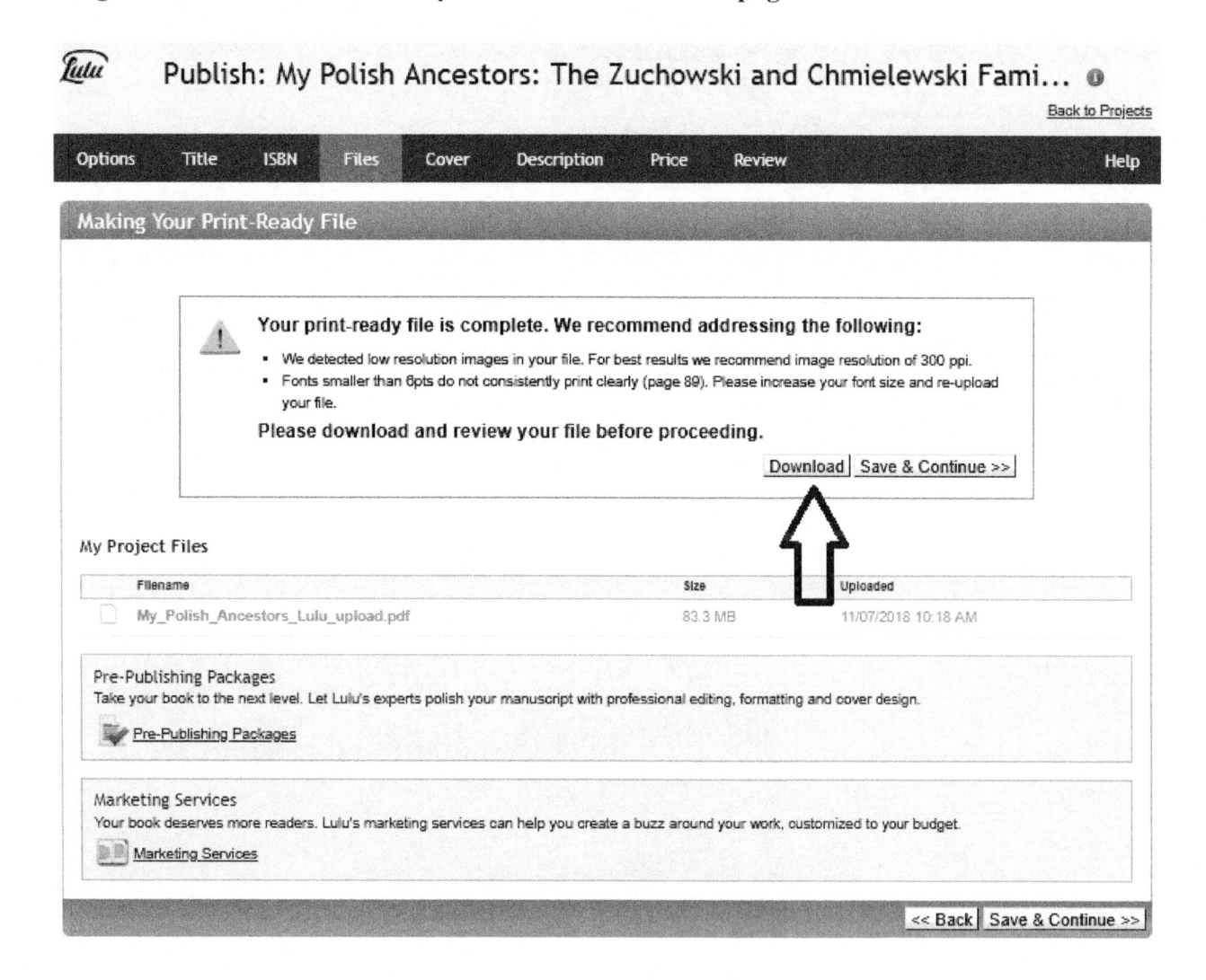

Below is the Lulu cover creator page. Lulu offers three options to create your cover. For updates to previous published books that used their old cover designer, click on the tab shown below. If you have a custom designed cover, you can upload using the advanced one-piece cover designer. I do not have the graphic software skills to create a custom cover so for family histories, I recommend using Lulu's new Cover Wizard. To access this cover creator, click "Get Flash" to load Adobe Flash player which you need for this tool.

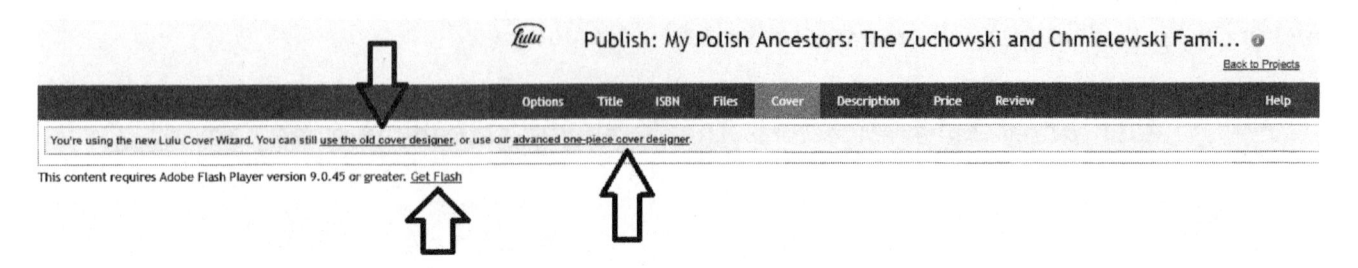

After you click on the cover tab, Lulu Cover Wizard loading icon (shown below) will appear. The example on the next page shows the Cover Wizard tabs to start your cover.

Lulu.com Example

Lulu offers custom options for the cover but I chose to use their cover creator and use one of their cover templates. The templates allowed me to upload my front cover picture, add text to sections of the back cover, change the theme, change the color and change the font. It was very easy to create a professional looking cover using their templates. Also the template can be changed at any time.

Below is an example of Lulu's Cover Creator Wizard page. The tabs in the middle of the top tool bar are used to design your cover. I use the background and layout tabs. First use the Themes tab to select how your cover looks. There are eighteen templates available. Next use the layout tab to select the format or layout of the cover, insert a picture, add the back cover text, and select the fonts for the text on the front and back covers. Use the background tab to select the colors of the front cover, back cover, and spine. The extras tab offers the option to add the Lulu logo on the spine and the Lulu URL on the back cover.

The zoom, fit, hide crop, preview, and full screen tabs are tools to improve your view of your cover as you are creating it.

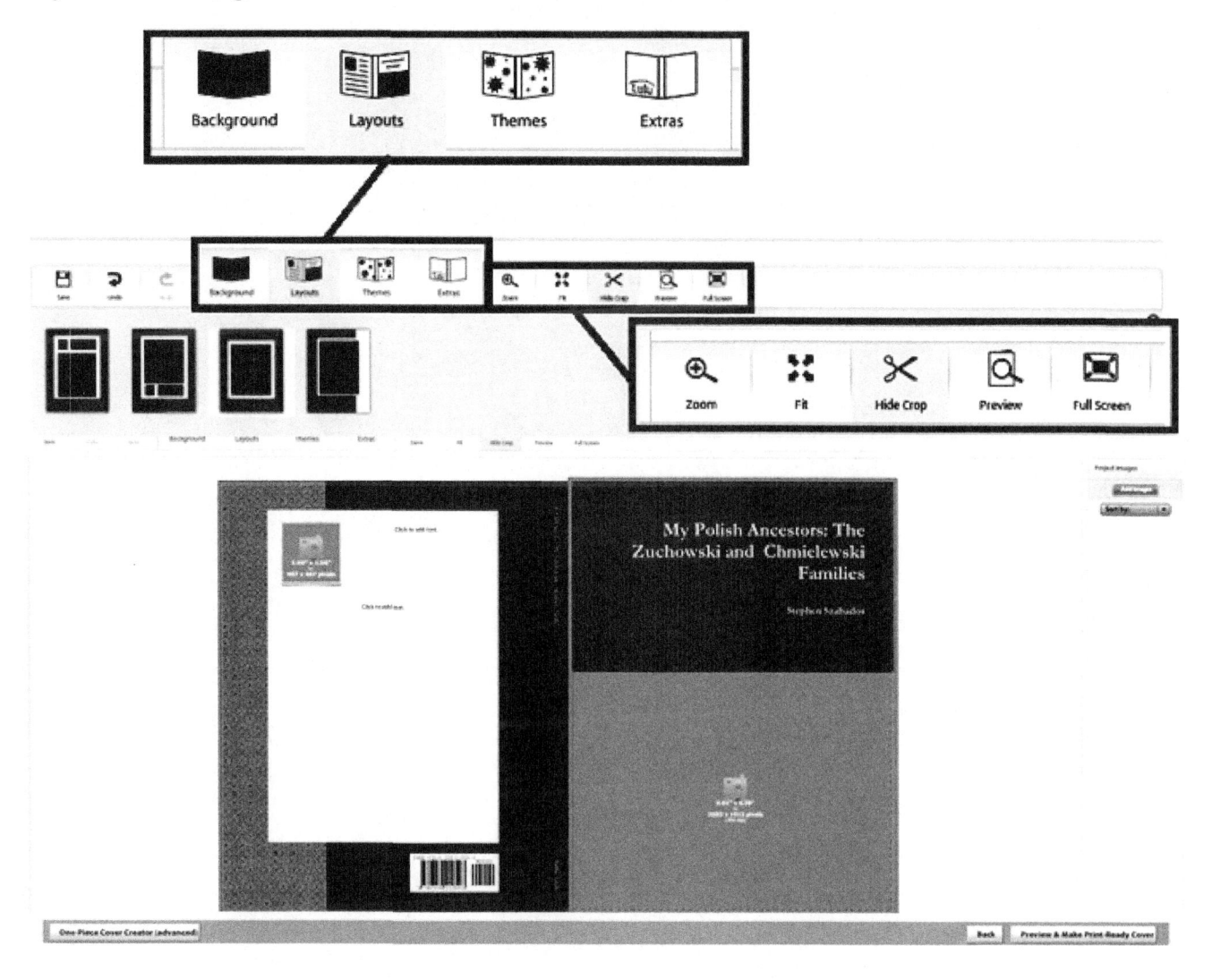

Select the "Theme" of your cover. Will there be a picture of the family on the front cover? Do you need a text box on the back cover? Will the back or front cover be multi-colored? There are eighteen templates.

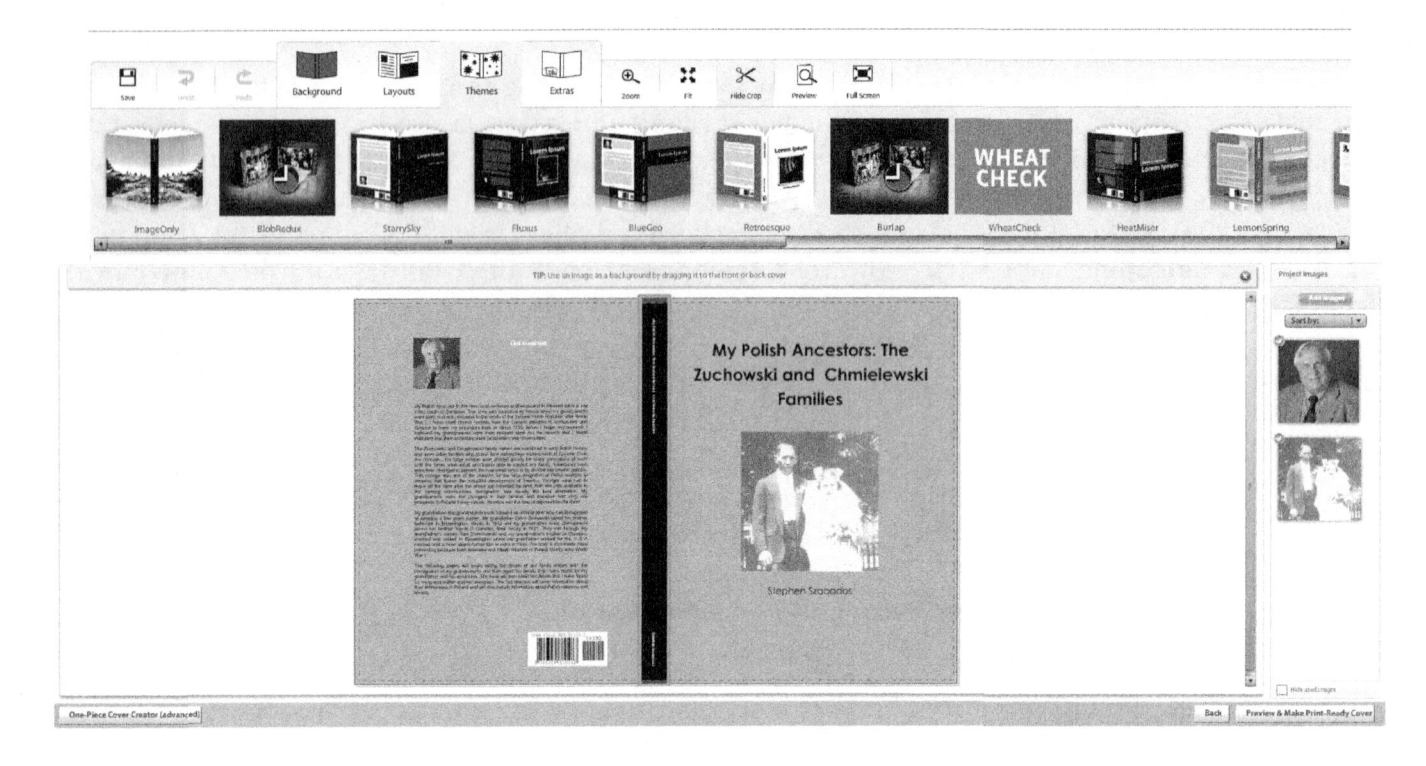

Lulu.com Example

Next select the layout of the different text and image boxes. The is page also allows images to be ulaod and then dragged to palce on the front or back covers. Add the text to the back cover that describes the content of the book. Then adjust the fonts for the text on the back cover, the title, and the author on the front cover.

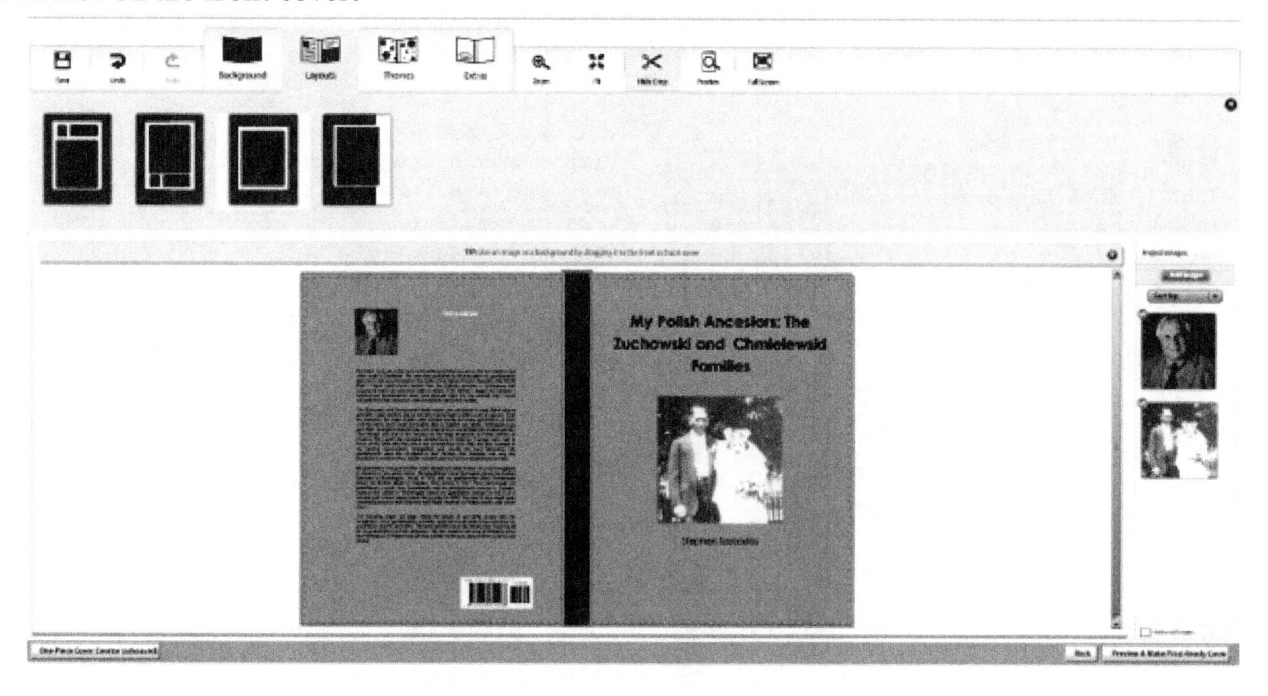

Next select the colors for the various areas. Select the area and then use the color pallet shown below to select the color.

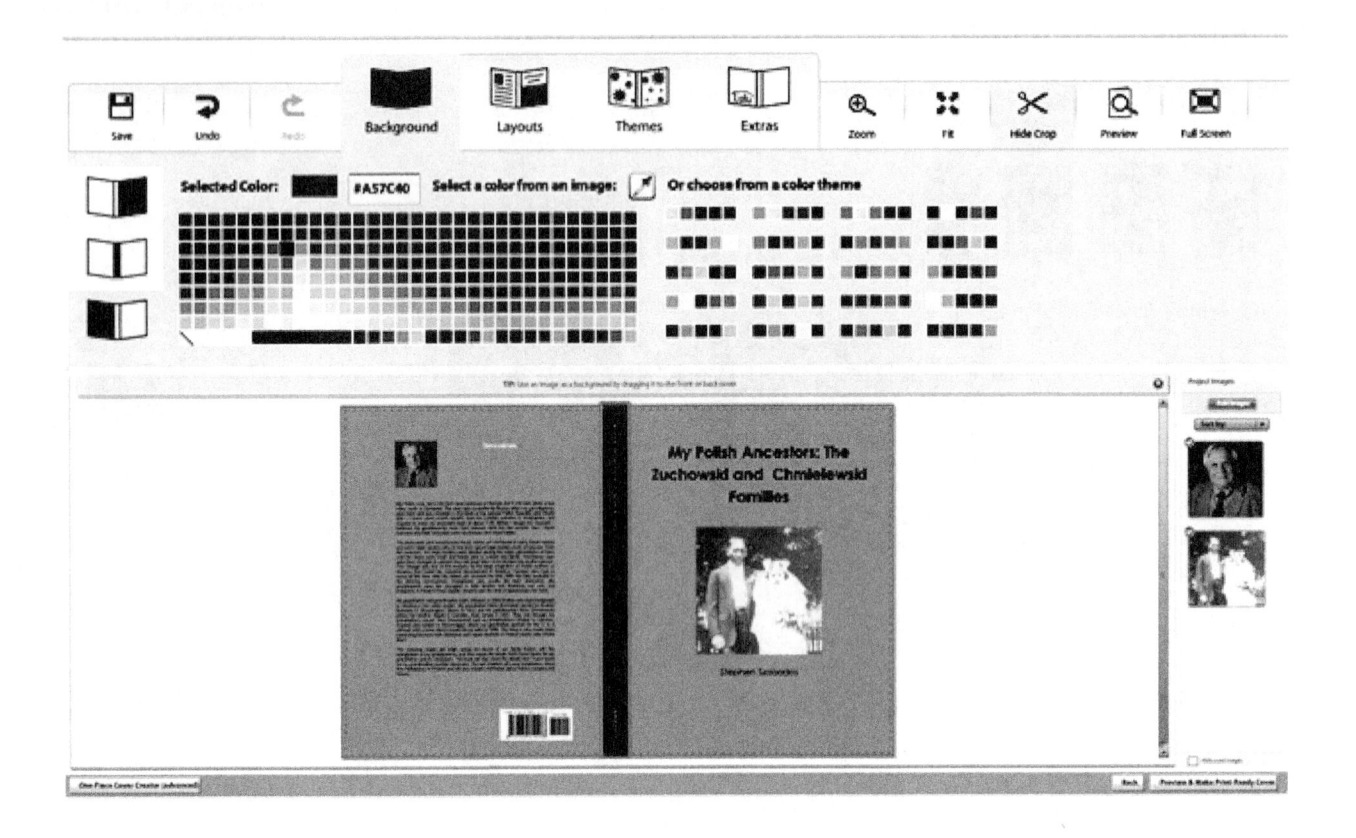

Lulu.com Example

When the cover is ready, click "Make Cover Print Ready" and then "Save & Continue."

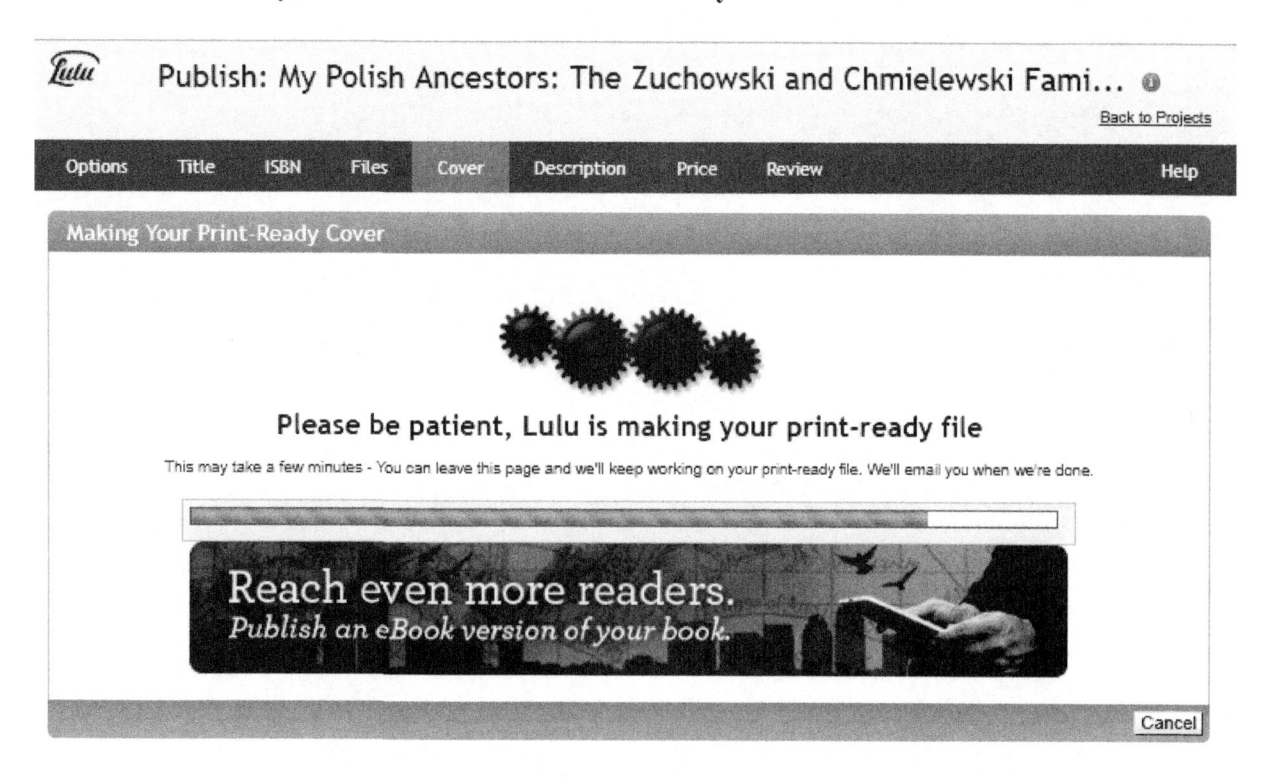

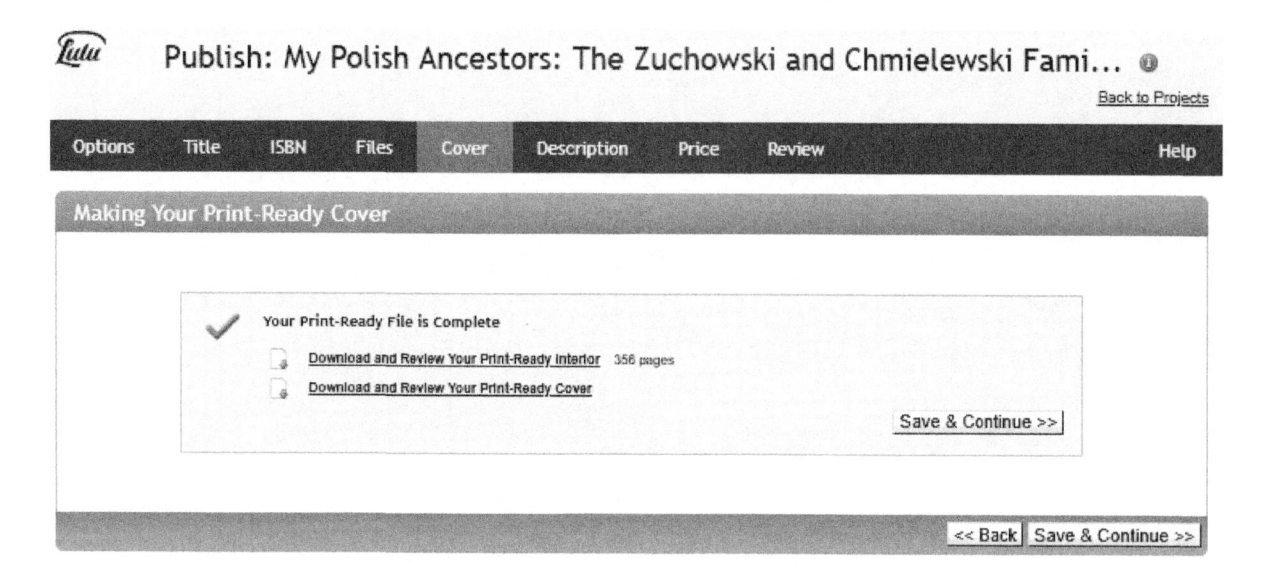

Writing Your Family History

The next step is to complete the setup of the book. This includes select Category, type in Keywords, add Description, and select License.

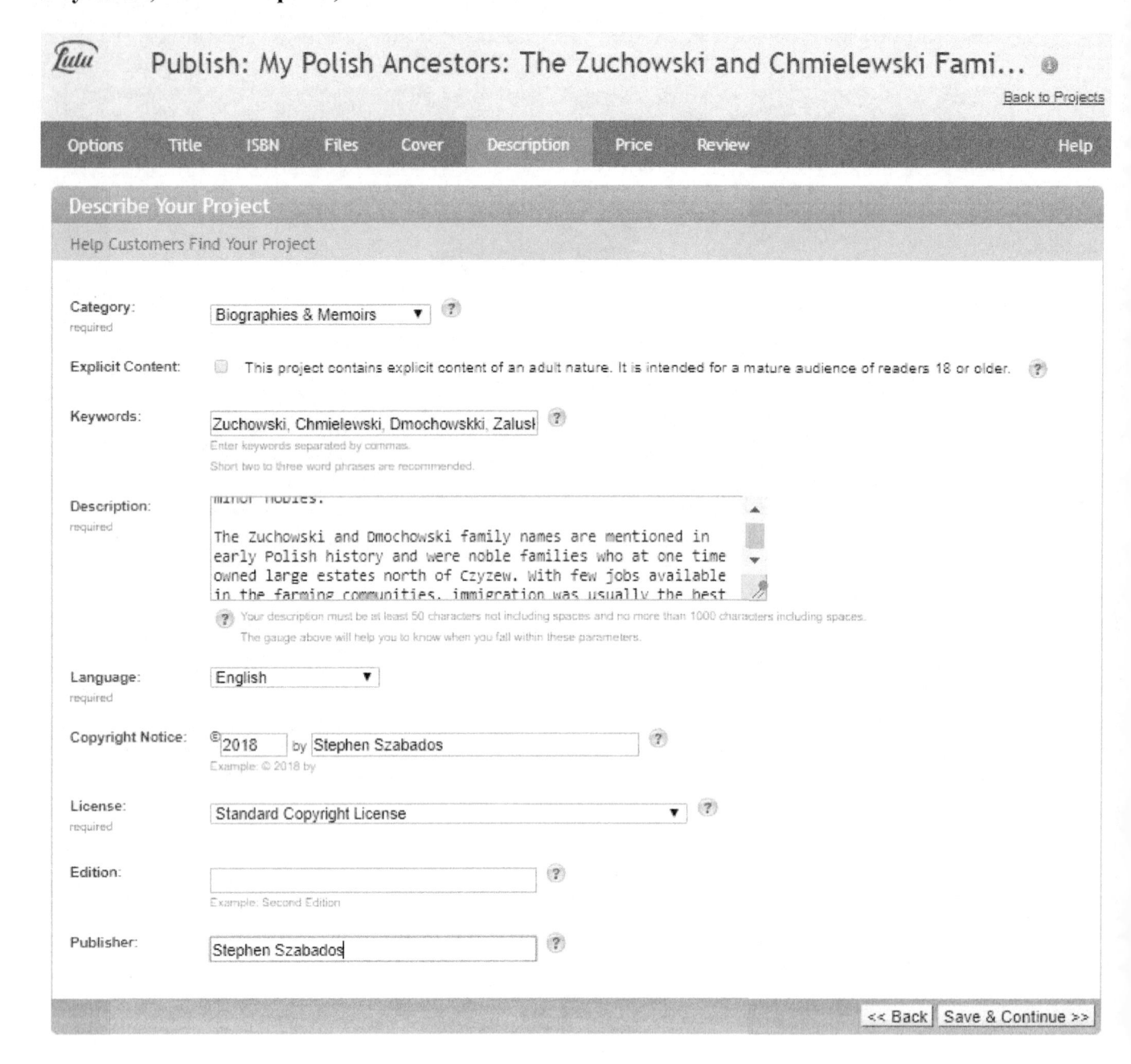

Lulu.com Example

The next click Save & Continue. On the next page setup a price for the book. This is a required step even if you plan to give your family all copies. Make sure the price you enter covers all of the costs and commissions due if your book is accidently sold on Lulu.

The price I set is cost plus a little extra amount. Below is an example showing that I set the price at $24.99 and the last column shows a royalty to me of $1.68. The minimum list price is shown at $21.00. The middle column shows a royalty of $11.13 and represents what you will net if a relative orders the book from the private web page for the book. The extra built into the price is in case I have made a mistake in my calculations. The only option to avoid charging your $21.oo is to setup distribution as "Private Access," and then you are the only person that can order copies.

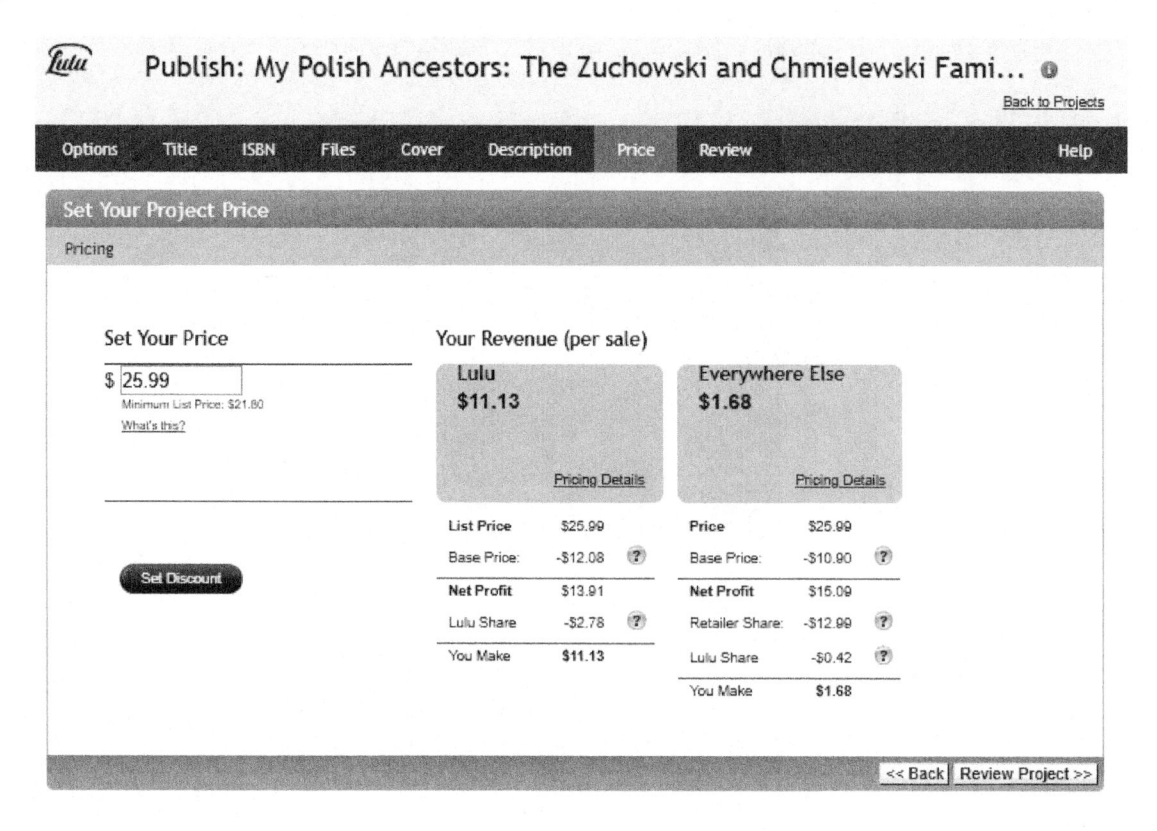

Next review the information for your project and make the final distribution decision: General, Direct, or Private. Below is an example of the Project Review Page and the example on the next page is a larger view of the portion in the lower right corner with the distribution options to select. After selection your preferred Distribution option and review all other information, click Save and finish.

AND YOU ARE DONE WITH THE SETUP OF YOUR FAMILY HISTORY>

"Review Your Project" Page

Lulu.com Example

Distribution Options

Pricing & License [Change]

Product	Price	Discounted	My Revenue	My Price
Retail Print	$25.99	—	$1.68	—
Print	$25.99	—	$11.13	$12.08

License: Standard Copyright License

Who Can View This on Lulu

○ Private Access
   — Available only to me

◉ **Direct Access**
   — Available only by private web address

○ General Access
   — Available through search and browse

APPENDIX C – USEFUL BOOKS AND WEBSITES

Books on Writing a Family History
- Banks, Keith E. - How to Write Your Personal and Family History, Heritage Books 2009 (General resource for personal and family history writing)
- Barnes, Nancy - Stories To Tell: An easy guide to self publishing family history books & memoirs, CreateSpace, 2010
- Carmack, Sharon DeBartolo - Organizing Your Family History Search, Betterway Books, Cincinnati, Ohio 1999
- Carmack, Sharon DeBartolo - You Can Write Your Family History, Betterway Books, Cincinnati, Ohio 2003 (Guide to writing your family history)
- Franco, Carol and Kent Lineback - The Legacy Guide: Capturing the Facts, Memories, and Meaning of Your Life. Tarcher, 2006
- Goldberg, Natalie - Writing Down the Bones, Shambhala, 2005
- Goldberg, Natalie - Old Friend from Far Away: The Practice of Writing Memoir, Atria Books, 2009
- Hatcher, Patricia Law - Producing a Quality Family History, Ancestry.com, 1996
- Hart, Cynthia and Lisa Samson - The Oral History Workshop: Collect and Celebrate the Life Stories of Your Family and Friends, Workman Publishing Company, 2009
- Kazemek, Francis - Exploring Our Lives: A Writing Handbook for Senior Adults, Santa Monica Press, 2002
- Kempthorne, Charley - For All Time, a Complete Guide to Writing Your Family History, Boynton/Cook Publishers, Portsmouth, New Hampshire 1996
- Kramer, Mark and Wendy Call edited by - Telling True Stories: A Nonfiction Writers' Guide from the Nieman Foundation at Harvard University, Plume, 2007
- Mills, Elizabeth Shown - QuickSheet Citing Online Historical Resources, Genealogical Publishing, Baltimore, Maryland 2007
- Mills, Elizabeth Shown - Evidence Explained : Citing History Sources From Artifacts To Cyberspace, Genealogical Publishing Company, Baltimore, Maryland, 2009
- Oliver, Laura. - The Story Within, ALPHA, 2011
- Polking, Kirk - Writing Family Histories and Memoirs, Writer's Digest Books (An outline of why and how to write different types of family histories, with brief information on basic research)
- Schawrz, Ted - The Complete Guide to Writing Biographies, Writers Digest Books, 1990
- Taylor, Maureen A. - Scrapbooking Your Family History,. Betterway Books, Cincinnati, Ohio 2003 (Organizing and preserving materials for family history based on memory books)
- Titford, John - Writing Up Your Family History, Countryside Books 2003 (Information on preparing, writing, and publishing your family history)

Writing Your Family History

Books on General Genealogy Research

- Allen, Desmond Walls - First Steps in Genealogy, Betterway Books, Cincinnati, Ohio 1998
- Bockman, Jeffrey A. - Give Your Family a Gift That Money Can't Buy, Alenjes publishing, Naperville, Illinois 2007
- Carmack, Sharon DeBartolo - Your Guide to Cemetery Research, Betterway Books, Cincinnati, Ohio 2002
- Carmack, Sharon DeBartolo - Guide to Finding Your Ellis Island Ancestors, Betterway Books, Cincinnati, Ohio 2005
- Colletta, John P. - They Came in Ships: A Guide to Finding Your Immigrant Ancestors Arrival Records, Ancestry, Salt Lake City, 1993
- Croom, Emily Anne - Unpuzzling Your Past, Betterway Books, Cincinnati, Ohio 2001
- Croom, Emily Anne - The Sleuth Book for Genealogists, Betterway Books, Cincinnati, Ohio 2000
- Croom, Emily Anne - The Genealogist's Companion & Sourcebook, Betterway Books, Cincinnati, Ohio 2003
- Fleming, Ann Carter - The Organized Family Historian, Rutledge Hill Press, Nashville, Tennessee 2004
- Hill, Richard - Richard Hill's Free Guide to DNA Testing, free at http://www.dna-testing-adviser.com/DNA-Testing-Guide.html
- Hinckley, Kathleen W. - Your Guide to the Federal Census, Betterway Books, Cincinnati, Ohio 1998
- Jones, Thomas W. - Mastering Genealogical Proof, National Genealogical Society, Inc., 2013
- Morgan, George G. and Drew Smith - Advanced Genealogy Research Techniques, McGraw-Hill Osborne Media; August 20, 2013
- Newman, John J. - American Naturalization Records 1790-1990: What They Are and How to Use Them, Heritage Quest, Bountiful, UT, 1998
- Quillen, W. Daniel - Mastering Census and Military Records, Cold Spring Press, 2011
- Quillen, W. Daniel - Secrets of Tracing Your Ancestors, Cold Spring Press, 2010
- Quillen, W. Daniel - Mastering Online Genealogy, Cold Spring Press, 2011
- Rising, Marsha Hoffman - The Family Tree Problem Solver, Family Tree Books, 2011
- Schaefer, Christina - Guide to Naturalization Records of the United States, Genealogical Publishing, Baltimore, 1997
- Spaltro, Kathleen - Genealogy and Indexing, Information Today, Medford, New Jersey 2003
- Szabados, Stephen – Basic Genealogy, Createspace 2013
- Szucs, Loretto Dennis - Finding Answers in U.S. Census Records, Ancestry Publishing, 2001
- Szucs, Loretto Dennis - They Became Americans: Finding Naturalization Records and Ethnic Origins, Ancestry, Salt Lake City, 1998
- U.S. Department of Justice - Foreign Variations and Diminutives of English Names, 1973

Useful Books and Websites

Useful Websites (free access unless $$ shown)
- Basic search - Family History Centers - http://www.familysearch.org
- Basic search - Ancestry.com ($$) or Ancestry Library Edition (free at local library) - http://www.ancestry.com/ (recommended for census records and passenger manifests)
- Basic research - ($$) - http://www.archives.com/
- Basic research - ($$) - http://genealogy.com/
- Basic research – Fold3 ($$) - http://www.fold3.com/
- Basic research - http://usgwarchives.net/
- Basic research - World Vital Records ($$) - http://www.worldvitalrecords.com/
- Basic research - Genealogy Trails - http://genealogytrails.com/
- Basic research - USGenweb Project - http://www.usgenweb.org/
- Cemetery records - Genealogy Trails History Group - http://genealogytrails.com/
- Cemetery records - http://www.findagrave.com/
- Cemetery records - http://www.interment.net/
- Cemetery records - Veterans Administration graves locator website - http://gravelocator.cem.va.gov
- Cemetery records - Iowa WPA cemetery website - http://iowawpagraves.org/
- Census & Military - ProQuest - http://www.proquest.com/ (available at many libraries)
- Directory - Cyndi's list - http://www.cyndislist.com/
- Education - Learn to interview - http://genealogy.about.com/cs/oralhistory/a/interview.htm
- Education - Familysearch.org/learningcenter
- Education - http://www.youtube.com/AncestryCom
- Education - http://genealogy.about.com/
- Immigration - Ellis Island Foundation - http://ellisisland.org/
- Immigration - Castle Garden - http://www.castlegarden.org/searcher.php
- Immigration & Military - U.S. National Archives - http://www.archives.gov/
- Land - Bureau of Land Management - http://www.glorecords.blm.gov/
- Message board - http://www.rootsweb.ancestry.com/
- Message board - http://Genforum.com
- Obituaries & News - Newspaperarchive - http://www.newspaperarchive.com/ ($$)
- Obituaries & News - NewsBank - http://www.newsbank.com/ (available at many libraries)
- Obituaries & News - Genealogy Bank - http://www.genealogybank.com/gbnk/ ($$)
- Obituaries & News - Godfrey Memorial Library - http://www.godfrey.org/ ($$)
- Search Utilities - http://stevemorse.org
- World War II resources - http://jenniferholik.com/world-war-ii-toolbox.html

INDEX

B
Birth records, 16, 51

C
Calumet Regional Archives, 35
Census Records, 13, 134
citing sources, 45
City directories, 15
copyright laws, 64
County Histories, 40
County Records, 37
court records, 39

D
Death Records, 36
Derivative sources, 50

E
eBook, 90
employment records, 33, 35
    Pullman-Standard Company, 34
exchange of information, 10
Exit Visas, 28

F
FamilyTree Maker, 4
farm directories, 15
footnotes, 45, 46

G
Genealogical Proof, 48

H
historical background, 55, 58

I
Immigration, 9, 23, 25, 83, 135

L
Land records, 37
Lulu.com, 89, 90, 91, 111

M
maps, 37, 67, 68, 77, 79, 86
Marriage records, 20
Military Records, 29

N
name changes
    myth of, 25
Naturalization papers, 25
Newberry Library, 35
Newspaper, 42

O
oral history, viii, 1, 2, 3, 7, 13, 29, 45, 54, 56, 59, 83
organize, viii, 4, 7, 12
Original sources, 49

P
passenger manifests, 23
photo albums, 1, 3
picture, ii, 2, 5, 7, 9, 11, 12, 13, 16, 20, 23, 55, 59, 67, 68, 69, 70, 74, 77, 79, 81, 83, 123
    inserting, 74
primary information, 50
print-on-demand, 89
Probate, 38

publish, 87
published family history, 43
publishing
    print-on-demand, 89

R
research log, 8, 12
ring binder, 4

S
secondary Information, 50
Smart Story, 4
social history, 55, 56, 58
South Suburban Genealogical Society, 34
Steerage Act of 1819, 23
summary, viii, ix, 4, 5, 7, 9, 10, 12, 14, 48, 53, 62, 65, 66, 81, 87, 90, 93, 111
summary format, 59
summary sample, 9
summary template, 9

T
timelines, 55, 56, 67, 81

V
Vital records
    birth, 16
    death, 36
    marriage, 20

W
where to start, 4
Why write, 1
Wills, 38, 67

ABOUT THE AUTHOR

Steve Szabados grew up in Central Illinois and is a retired project manager living in the Chicago Suburbs. He received a Bachelor of Science Degree from the University of Illinois in Champaign-Urbana, Illinois and a Masters in Business Administration from Northern Illinois University in DeKalb, Illinois.

He has been researching his ancestors since 2000 and has traced ancestors back to the 1600s in New England and the 1730's in Poland, Germany, Bohemia, Hungary, Slovakia and Slovenia. He has given numerous presentations to genealogical groups and libraries in Illinois, Indiana, Michigan, Missouri, Pennsylvania and Wisconsin. His mission is to share his passion for Family History with as many people as he can. He is a member of the Northwest Suburban Genealogy Society and Illinois State Genealogical Society. He was a board member of Polish Genealogical Society of America and he is a genealogy volunteer at the Arlington Heights Memorial Library. Steve also is the genealogy columnist for the Polish American Journal.

Printed in Great Britain
by Amazon